Access 2000
fast&easy™

Send Us Your Comments

To comment on this book or any other PRIMA TECH title, visit our reader response page on the Web at **www.prima-tech.com/comments**.

How to Order

For information on quantity discounts, contact the publisher: Prima Publishing, P.O. Box 1260BK, Rocklin, CA 95677-1260; (916) 632-4400. On your letterhead, include information concerning the intended use of the books and the number of books you wish to purchase. For individual orders, visit PRIMA TECH's Web site at **www.prima-tech.com**.

Access 2000
fast&easy™

Patrice-Anne Rutledge

A DIVISION OF PRIMA PUBLISHING

A Division of Prima Publishing

Prima Publishing and colophon are registered trademarks of Prima Communications, Inc. PRIMA TECH and Fast & Easy are trademarks of Prima Communications, Inc., Rocklin, California 95677.

Publisher: Stacy L. Hiquet

Associate Publisher: Nancy Stevenson

Managing Editor: Dan J. Foster

Senior Acquisitions Editor: Deborah F. Abshier

Project Editor: Kevin W. Ferns

Assistant Project Editor: Estelle Manticas

Technical Reviewer: Elizabeth Reding

Novice Reviewer: Jim Terry

Copy Editor: Suzanne Stone

Interior Layout: Marian Hartsough

Cover Design: Prima Design Team

Indexer: Katherine Stimson

Microsoft, Windows, Windows NT, Outlook, MSN, and FrontPage are trademarks or registered trademarks of Microsoft Corporation.

Important: If you have problems installing or running Microsoft Access, go to Microsoft's Web site at **www.microsoft.com**. Prima Publishing cannot provide software support.

ISBN: 0-7615-1404-X

Library of Congress Catalog Card Number: 98-68146

Printed in the United States of America

99 00 01 02 03 DD 10 9 8 7 6 5 4 3 2 1

To my family,
with thanks for your love and support

Acknowledgments

I'd like to thank all the people at Prima Publishing who contributed to the creation of this book. To Debbie Abshier for suggesting that I write this book; to Kevin Ferns for his many organizational and editorial contributions; and to Estelle Manticas, Jim Terry, and Liz Reding for their attention to detail.

And special thanks to my mom, Phyllis Rutledge, for both her editorial expertise and her encouragement throughout this project.

About the Author

PATRICE-ANNE RUTLEDGE is a computer consultant and author based near San Francisco. She has written on a variety of topics, including technology, business, and travel, and has authored or co-authored 18 computer books on topics such as Microsoft Office and Microsoft Publisher. She wrote the highly-acclaimed *Access 97 Fast & Easy*, as well as *The Essential Publisher 97 Book*, also published by Prima Tech. As an independent consultant and a member of the IS team for various international technology firms, Patrice has been involved in many aspects of computing, including software development, training, and technical communications. Patrice initially discovered computers while pursuing a career as a technical translator and quickly changed the focus of her career. She holds a degree in French Linguistics from the University of California and has been working with Access for more than six years.

Contents at a Glance

Contents

Introduction

Access 2000 is one of the world's most popular relational database systems, and it's part of the Microsoft Office 2000 Professional Edition. Using Access, you can create sophisticated and powerful databases to store and analyze information on any number of topics. For many beginning computer users, however, database programs seem complicated and intimidating. But they needn't be.

Access 2000 Fast & Easy isn't designed to provide comprehensive coverage on every aspect of Access. Instead, it focuses on the best way to do essential tasks and provides step-by-step visual instructions on how to do these tasks. Using this approach makes creating a database both fast and easy.

Who Should Read This Book?

Access 2000 Fast & Easy is a visual guide, created for people who learn best by seeing a representation of what they're doing. This book is directed at beginning to intermediate computer users, particularly those new to Access 2000. More experienced users who prefer a visual, hands-on approach may also benefit from this book. If you want to look and learn without having to wade through a lot of text and technical detail, then this book is for you.

Added Advice to Make You a Pro

Access 2000 Fast & Easy provides a step-by-step, sequential approach to learning. Starting at the very beginning, the book guides you through the creation of an entire relational database system. Along the way, you'll discover several elements that help you increase your knowledge and proficiency.

- **Tips** provide hints on ways to make common tasks even easier or suggest shortcuts for these tasks.

- **Notes** offer useful background information, advice, or suggestions that will help you learn more about the program.

- **Cautions** keep you on your toes by notifying you of potential pitfalls and hazards that might hinder your progress.

Finally, the appendixes will help you install the software and utilize some of the popular keystroke shortcuts available.

I hope you enjoy reading and using *Access 2000 Fast & Easy*!

PART I

Getting Started

1

Welcome to Access

Access 2000 is one of the most popular and powerful database applications available. Using Access, you can easily create a relational database that includes data entry forms, reports, and queries. In this chapter, you'll learn how to:

- Start Access
- Exit Access

Starting Access

Depending on the options you choose when you install Access 2000, the menu path you use to start Access may differ slightly.

1. **Click** on the **Start button**, located in the lower-left corner of the screen. The Start menu will appear.

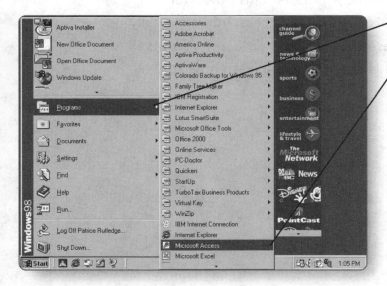

2. **Click** on **Programs**. The Program menu will appear.

3. **Click** on **Microsoft Access**.

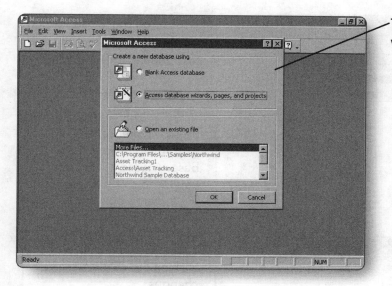

The Microsoft Access window will open.

Exiting Access

When you finish working in Access, be sure to exit the program properly to avoid damaging your database.

1. Click on **File**. The File menu will appear.

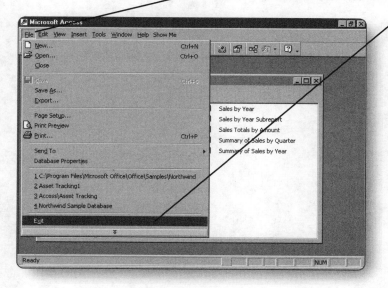

2a. Click on **Exit**. Access 2000 will close and you will return to the Windows desktop.

OR

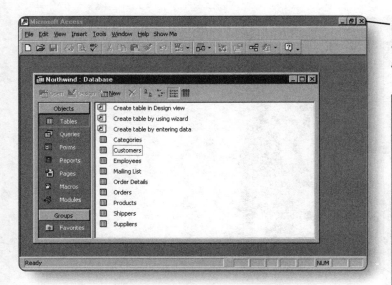

2b. Click on the **Close button** as an alternate way to exit Access 2000 in only one step.

TIP

If you haven't saved everything in your database, Access will prompt you to do so by displaying a dialog box that asks whether you want to save your changes. Click on Yes to save the changes; click on No to discard the changes.

2

Working with Access

Before you create your first Access database, you need to know how to use menus, toolbars, and dialog boxes, and how to get help when you need it. Fortunately, all of this will be familiar if you already use other Windows 95 or 98 programs, particularly other Office 2000 applications. In this chapter, you'll learn how to:

- Use menus
- Use toolbars
- Work with dialog boxes
- Get help using Access

Using Menus

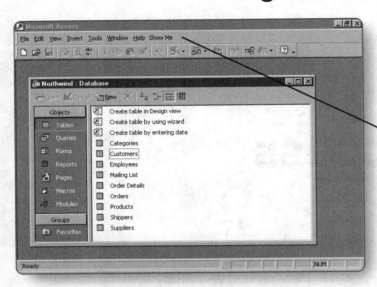

You need to issue commands in order to use Access. Menus are one of the most common ways to issue commands and navigate in Access.

The menu bar, directly below the Access title bar, includes several menu option names that open groups of menu commands. Depending on where you are in Access and what you're doing, the menu structure will change, providing appropriate menu options.

Opening a Menu

1. Click on **File**. A menu of available commands will appear.

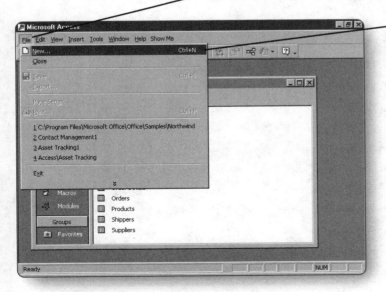

2. Click on the **menu command** you want to perform, such as New.

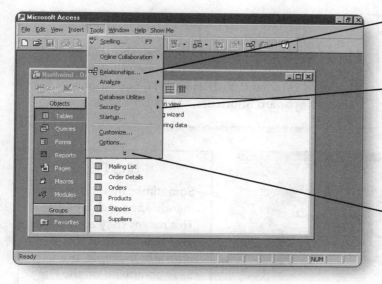

When you click on a menu command that is followed by an ellipsis, a dialog box will open.

When you click on a menu command that is followed by a right arrow, another menu will appear. Then, click on a command in that menu to perform the command.

Menus initially display only the most commonly used menu commands. To view additional commands, click on the double down arrows at the bottom of a menu.

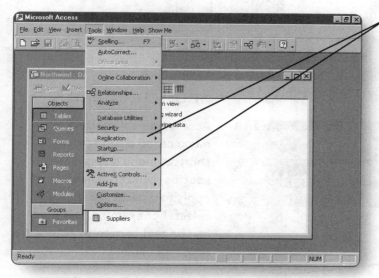

The menu then displays additional, hidden menu choices. Click on the one you need, and the next time you open the menu it won't be hidden.

TIP

Many Access menu com-mands have shortcut keys. A shortcut key lets you bypass the menu by pressing a keyboard command such as Ctrl+N. See Appendix B, "Using Keyboard Shortcuts," for a list of these keys.

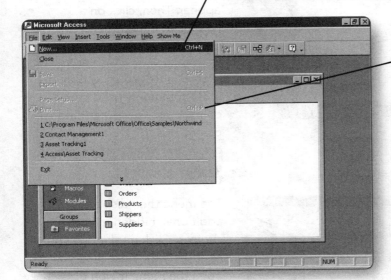

NOTE

Sometimes menu commands appear dimmed. This means they aren't available to use at this time. For example, the Save command on the File menu will appear dimmed if you haven't created new data.

Using a Shortcut Menu

Access offers a special kind of menu called a shortcut menu. A shortcut menu displays the specific menu commands that apply to a particular item you select. For example, this item can be text, a graphic object, a row, or a column.

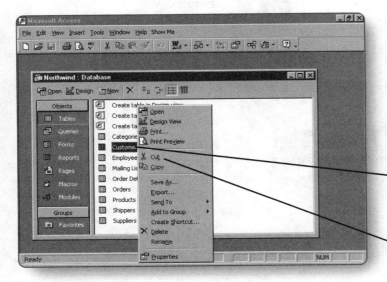

1. Right-click on the **item** whose shortcut menu you want to see. The menu will appear.

2. Click on the **menu command** to perform it.

Using Toolbars

Toolbars make it easy to use the program's most common features and functions. If you use other Office applications, such as Word or Excel, some of these toolbars and buttons may look familiar; there are many similarities among the Office products.

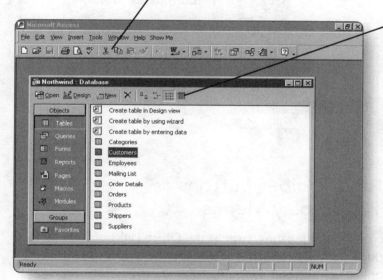

When you click on a button on the toolbar, you either perform a command or open a dialog box. When Access displays a database window, you see the Database toolbar. As you open individual tables, queries, forms, and reports within that database, the toolbars change. For example, when you open a table, the Table Datasheet toolbar appears and the Database toolbar disappears.

Finding Out What a Toolbar Button Does

You can use the Access ScreenTips feature to find out what a particular toolbar button does.

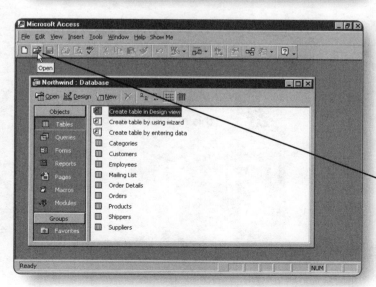

Hover the mouse over the button without clicking on it. A ScreenTip will appear describing what the button does.

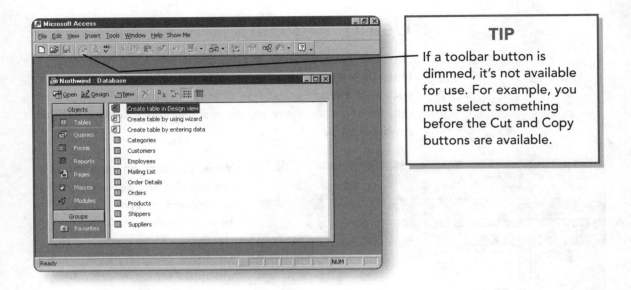

TIP

If a toolbar button is dimmed, it's not available for use. For example, you must select something before the Cut and Copy buttons are available.

Using Toolbar Buttons That Display Menus

Some toolbar buttons, such as the Office Links or New Object buttons on the Standard toolbar, include a down arrow to the right of the button that opens a menu.

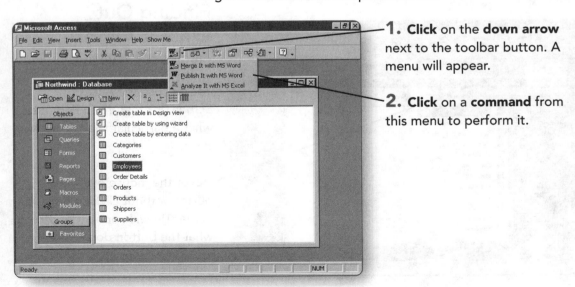

1. **Click** on the **down arrow** next to the toolbar button. A menu will appear.

2. **Click** on a **command** from this menu to perform it.

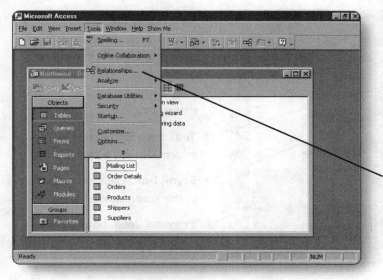

Working with Dialog Boxes

You'll use dialog boxes frequently in Access to make choices, issue commands, and apply formatting.

When you click on a menu command followed by an ellipsis, a dialog box opens. The name of the dialog box appears in the title bar.

Dialog boxes can contain any of the following elements:

- **Option button**. Click on the option button to select that option. You can only select one option in a group of option buttons.

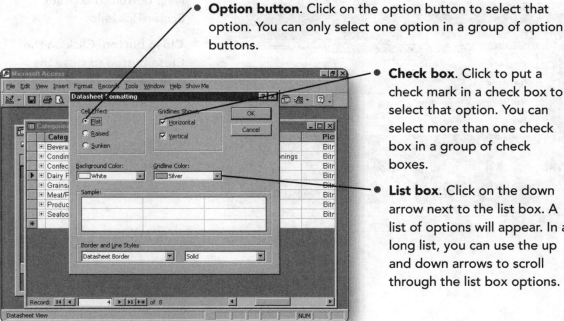

- **Check box**. Click to put a check mark in a check box to select that option. You can select more than one check box in a group of check boxes.

- **List box**. Click on the down arrow next to the list box. A list of options will appear. In a long list, you can use the up and down arrows to scroll through the list box options.

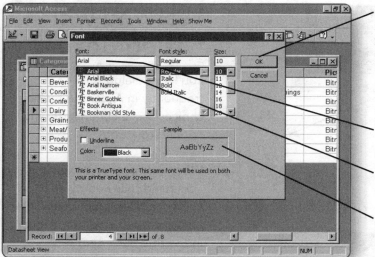

- **Command button**. Click on a command button to perform the command. A command button that includes an ellipsis will open a secondary dialog box.

- **Text box**. Enter data or information in a text box.

- **Scroll box**. Click on an option in the scroll box to select it.

- **Preview area**. Look at the preview area to view how your choices will appear.

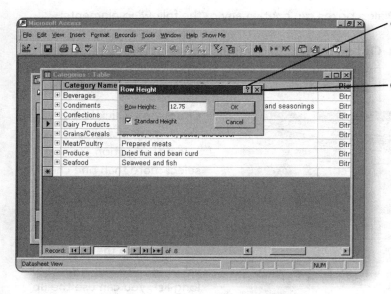

- **Help button**. Click on the Help button to activate ScreenTips help.

- **Close button**. Click on the Close button to close the dialog box.

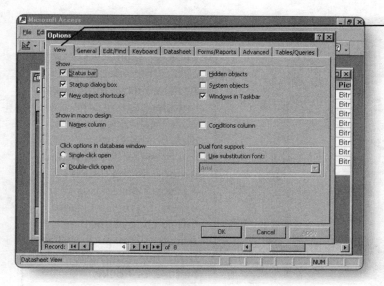

• **Tab**. Click on a Tab to move to another sheet in the dialog box.

Getting Help

Access provides several ways of getting help if you have a problem using the program. These help features include the Office Assistant, which enables you to ask questions and get answers; the Microsoft Access Help window, which includes a detailed help index; and the What's This? command, which enables you to point to an object or area and ask what it is.

TIP

If the Office Assistant doesn't appear, it may be hidden. To display the Office Assistant again, click on Help, Show the Office Assistant from the menu bar.

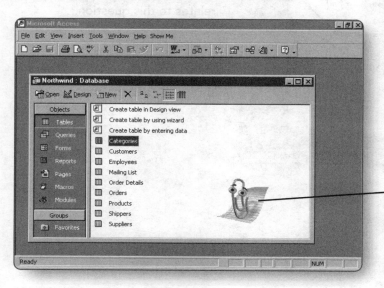

Using the Office Assistant

The Office Assistant appears automatically. It provides context-sensitive help and lets you ask questions about a task you want to perform.

1. Click on the **Office Assistant**. The Office Assistant message balloon will appear.

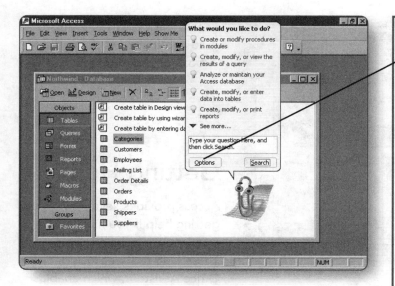

NOTE

Clipit (an animated paperclip) is the default Office Assistant icon, but Access includes several others as well. To change the icon, click on the Options button in the Office Assistant balloon. In the Office Assistant dialog box that opens, go to the Gallery tab to choose another Assistant icon such as The Dot, The Genius, Mother Nature, or Rocky.

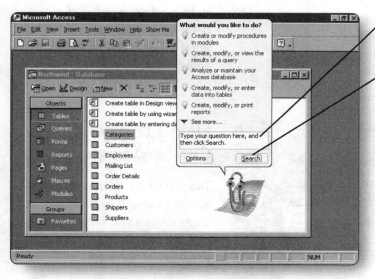

2. Enter a **specific question** in the text box.

3. Click on the **Search button**. A new topic list will appear that relates to this question.

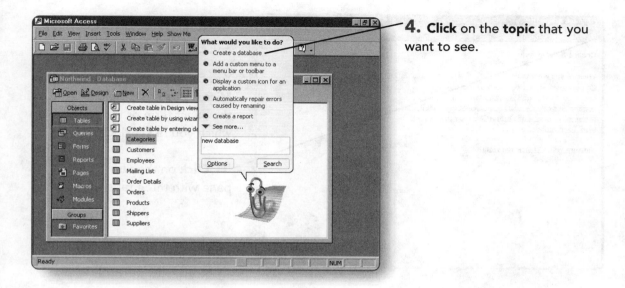

4. Click on the **topic** that you want to see.

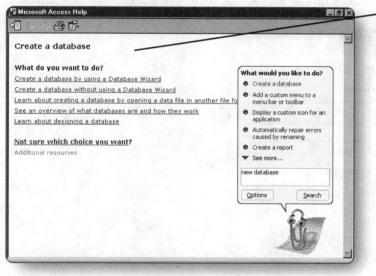

The Microsoft Access Help window for this topic will appear.

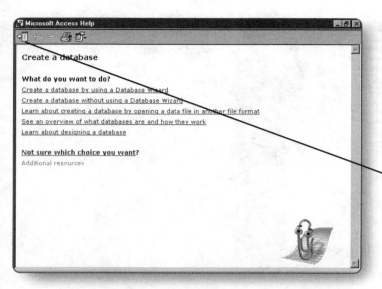

Using the Microsoft Access Help Index

You can also search the Microsoft Access Help index for the exact term or topic for which you're seeking help.

1. Click on the **Show button**. A pane with three tabs will appear.

2. Click on the **Index tab**. A complete help index will appear.

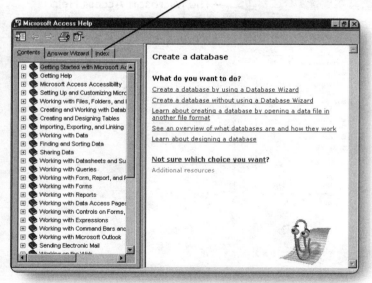

3a. **Enter** the **topic** you want to search for in the Type Keywords text box. The index will move to this entry.

OR

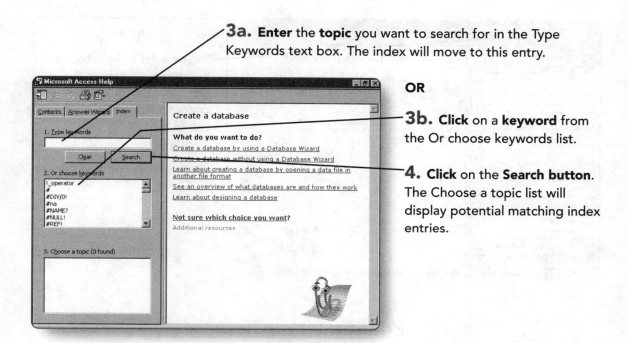

3b. **Click** on a **keyword** from the Or choose keywords list.

4. **Click** on the **Search button**. The Choose a topic list will display potential matching index entries.

5. **Click** on the **index entry** you want to view.

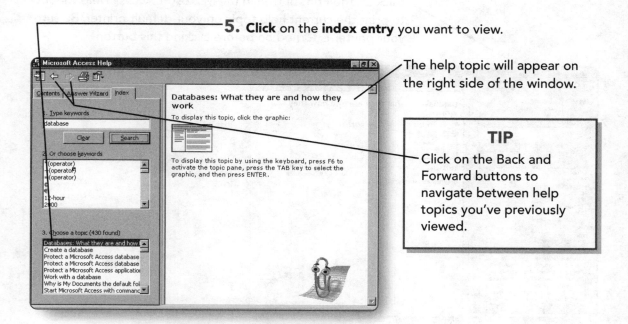

The help topic will appear on the right side of the window.

TIP

Click on the Back and Forward buttons to navigate between help topics you've previously viewed.

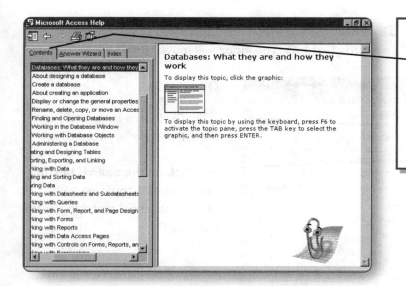

TIP

To see a list of help topics by category, click on the Contents tab. A table of contents listing the help topics by category will display.

Printing a Help Topic

Click on the Print button in the Microsoft Access Help window to print the current help topic on your default printer. Be sure your printer is turned on before clicking this button.

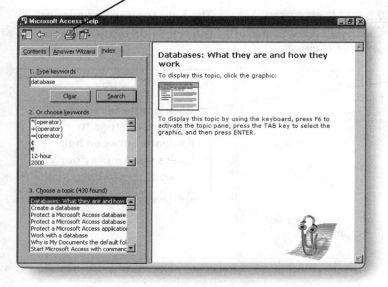

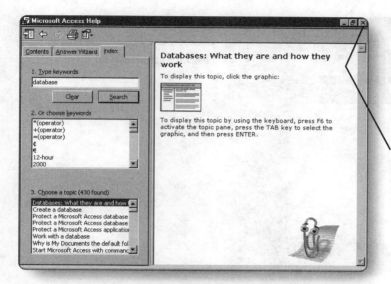

Exiting Help

After you find the help information you need, you can exit the help system and return to Access.

Click on the Close button to exit Microsoft Access Help.

Hiding the Office Assistant

Sometimes the Office Assistant just seems to get in the way on the Access desktop. You can hide it from view until the next time you need it.

1. Click on **Help**. The Help menu will open.

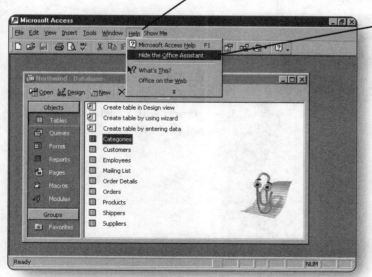

2. Click on **Hide the Office Assistant**. The Office Assistant will be hidden from view.

TIP

You can also right-click on the Assistant and choose Hide from the shortcut menu that displays.

To display the Assistant again, click on the Microsoft Access Help toolbar button.

Using What's This? to Get Help

Access includes a feature called What's This? Using this feature, you can access a ScreenTip for a menu command, toolbar button, or other item on the screen.

1. Click on **Help**. The Help menu will appear.

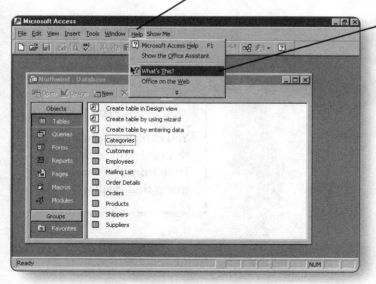

2. Click on **What's This?** What's This? will be activated.

3. Click on the **toolbar button**, **menu command**, or **part of the screen** with which you want help.

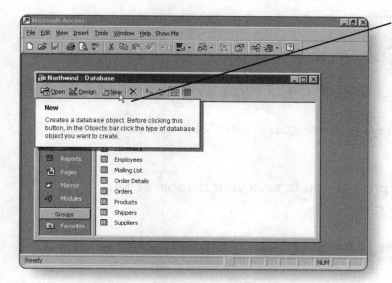

A ScreenTip will appear, providing basic information about the item you selected.

Using What's This? in a Dialog Box

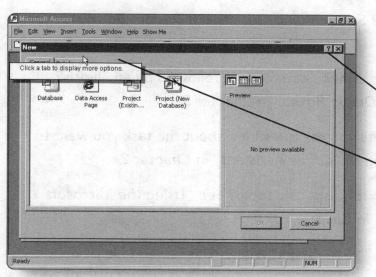

You can also access What's This? from a dialog box, but the steps are a little different.

1. Click on the **? button** in the upper-right corner of the dialog box to activate What's This?

2. Click on the **part** of the **dialog box** with which you need help. The ScreenTip will appear.

Part I Review Questions

1. How do you open Access 2000? *See "Starting Access" in Chapter 1*

2. What are the two ways to exit Access? *See "Exiting Access" in Chapter 1*

3. When does Access prompt you to save your database? *See "Exiting Access" in Chapter 1*

4. What is the best way to navigate Access? *See "Using Menus" in Chapter 2*

5. Which menu lets you see commands that apply only to the item you select? *See "Using a Shortcut Menu" in Chapter 2*

6. What's a ScreenTip? *See "Finding Out What a Toolbar Button Does" in Chapter 2*

7. What happens when a menu command is followed by an ellipsis? *See "Working with Dialog Boxes" in Chapter 2*

8. What help option lets you ask questions about the task you want to perform? *See "Using the Office Assistant" in Chapter 2*

9. How can you search for a specific topic? *See "Using the Microsoft Access Help Index" in Chapter 2*

10. What's "What's This?" *See "Using What's This? to Get Help" in Chapter 2*

PART II

Working with Databases

3

Creating a Database

Using the Access Database Wizard, you can quickly create detailed databases that handle a number of business and personal functions such as order entry, contact management, or event management. If none of the database templates in the Database Wizard suits your needs or if you just want to create a database from scratch, you can easily do so as well. In this chapter, you'll learn how to:

- Start the Database Wizard
- Use the Database Wizard
- Create a blank database when you first start Access
- Create a blank database from within Access

Starting the Database Wizard When You First Begin Access

When you first start Access, you can create a database using the Database Wizard option in the Microsoft Access dialog box. This dialog box automatically appears when you start the program.

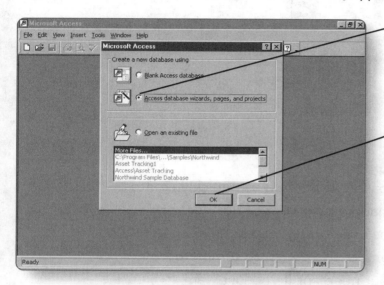

1. Click on the **Access database wizards, pages, and projects option button** in the initial Microsoft Access dialog box.

2. Click on **OK**. The New dialog box will open.

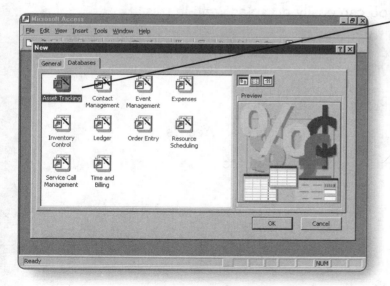

Icons for the available database templates will appear under the Databases tab.

Starting the Database Wizard from within Access

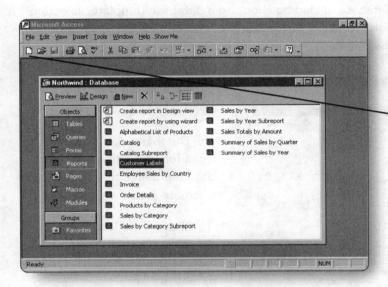

If you are already working in Access, you will follow slightly different steps to start the Database Wizard.

1. Click on the **New Database button**. The New dialog box will open.

2. Click on the **Databases tab**. Icons for the available database templates will appear.

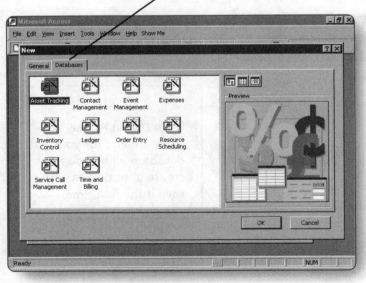

Using the Database Wizard

The Database Wizard guides you through the creation of a database, including choosing a database template, selecting fields, making customizations, adding pictures, and finishing the database.

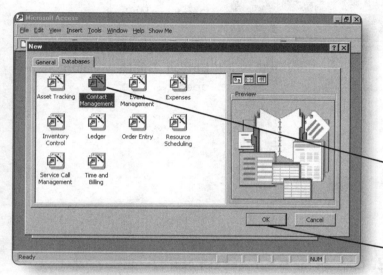

Choosing a Database Template

The Databases tab includes icons for many different database templates that you can use to create your own database.

1. Click on the **icon** for the database template that you want to use as the basis for your database.

2. Click on **OK**. The File New Database dialog box will open.

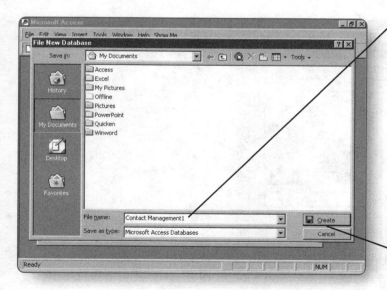

3. Enter a **name** for the new database in the File name text box.

TIP

Note that in Access you enter a name for your database when you first create it, not when you save it the first time.

---

4. Click on **Create**. The Database Wizard will open.

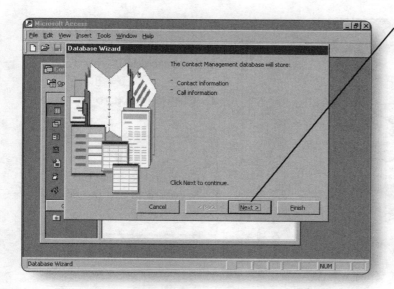

5. Click on **Next** to continue.

Selecting Database Fields

A database can contain one or more tables, each with numerous fields.

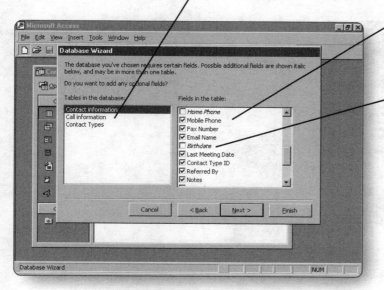

The fields you'll probably want to have in your tables are already selected.

Additional fields that you may want to consider are not automatically selected, and are listed in italics.

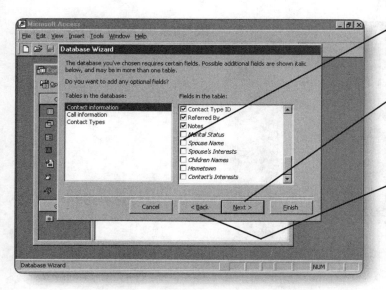

1. **Click** on the **check box** next to any additional field that you want to include in your table.

2. **Click** on **Next** to continue.

TIP

Click on the Back button to return to the previous wizard step.

Customizing the Database

Next, you'll customize your database by choosing styles for screens and reports. You'll also add a title to your database.

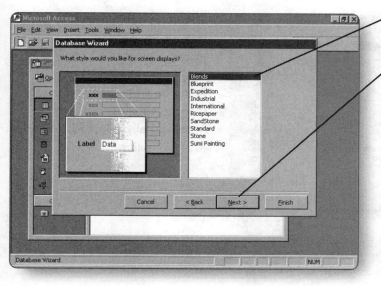

1. **Click** on the **style** that you want to use in database screens.

2. **Click** on **Next** to continue.

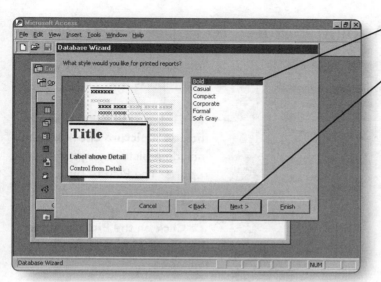

3. **Click** on the **style** that you want to use in printed reports.

4. **Click** on **Next**.

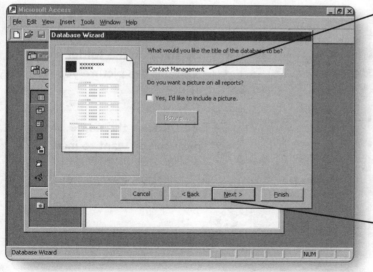

5. **Enter** the **title of your database** in the text box.

NOTE

This is the title that appears on database objects—not the name for the database itself.

6. **Click** on **Next**.

Adding Pictures to Reports

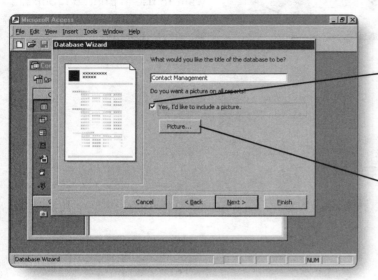

You can also add pictures to your reports.

1. Click on the **Yes, I'd like to include a picture check box** to include a picture on your reports. The Picture button will activate.

2. Click on the **Picture button**. The Insert Picture dialog box will open.

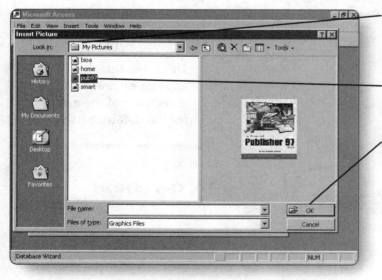

3. Click on the **folder** that contains the picture you want to insert.

4. Click on the **name of the picture** you want to insert.

5. Click on **OK**.

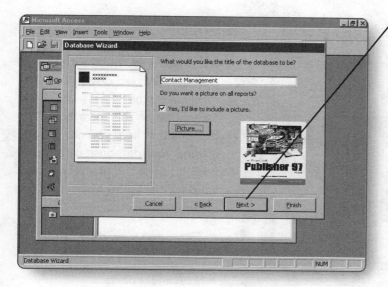

6. Click on **Next** to continue.

Finishing the Database

1. Click on the **Yes, start the database check box** to start the database when you finish the Database Wizard.

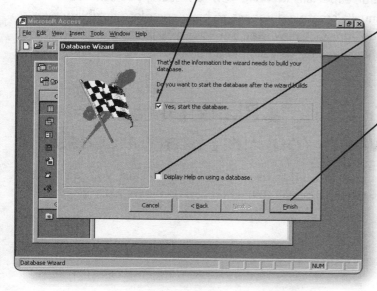

2. Click on the **Display Help on using a database check box** to activate online help when you begin using the database.

3. Click on **Finish**. The Database Wizard will build the database.

Viewing Your Database

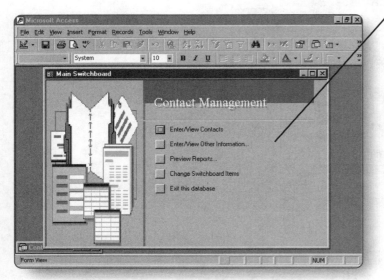

A database you build with the Database Wizard displays a form called the Main Switchboard. This form includes buttons that help you navigate around your database without having to use the main database window. Using the Main Switchboard you can:

- Enter and view data using forms

- Preview reports

- Change switchboard items

- Exit the database

Although using a database with a main switchboard can be useful, especially if you're new to Access, you can also manually create a database to have complete flexibility over its design. As a new user, however, you probably will want to manually create very simple databases, at least at first.

Creating a Blank Database When You First Start Access

If you don't want to use the Database Wizard, you can create a database from scratch when you first start Access.

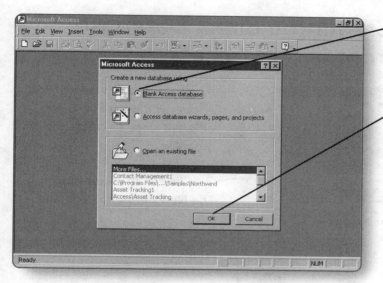

1. **Click** on the **Blank Access database option button** in the initial Microsoft Access dialog box.

2. **Click** on **OK**. The File New Database dialog box will open.

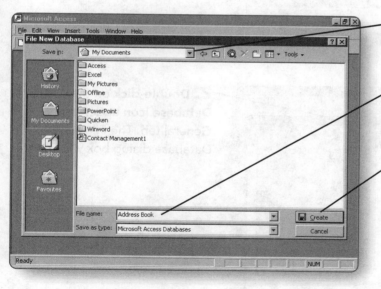

3. **Click** on the **folder** in which you want to store your new database.

4. **Enter** an **appropriate name** for the database in the File name text box.

5. **Click** on **Create**. A blank database will appear in your Access window.

Creating a Blank Database from within Access

If you are already working in Access, you will follow slightly different steps to create a blank database.

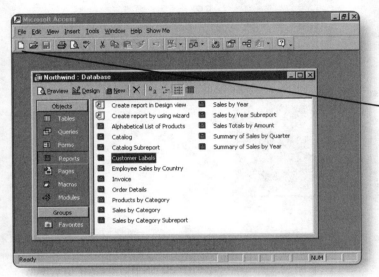

1. Click on the **New button**. The New dialog box will open.

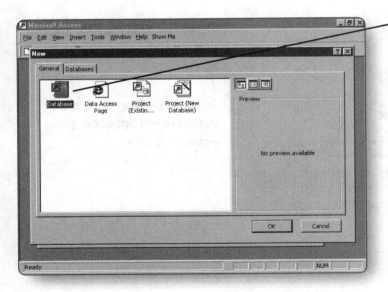

2. Double-click on the **Database icon** under the General tab. The File New Database dialog box will open.

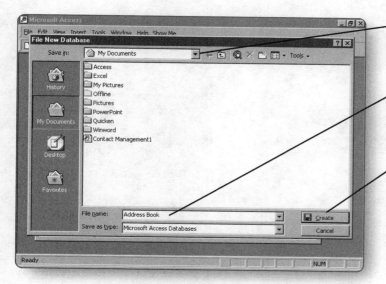

3. Click on the **folder** in which you want to store your new database.

4. Enter an **appropriate name** for the database in the File name text box.

5. Click on **Create**. A blank database will appear in your Access window. You can now develop tables, forms, queries, and reports.

4

Opening and Using Databases

Once you create a database in Access, you'll want to open it again and again. You'll also need to familiarize yourself with the Database Window before you start working with tables, reports, queries, and forms within the database. In this chapter, you'll learn how to:

- Open an existing database
- Understand the Database Window
- Use the Database Window

Opening an Existing Database

You can open an existing Access database from the initial Microsoft Access dialog box.

1. Click on the **Open an existing file option button**.

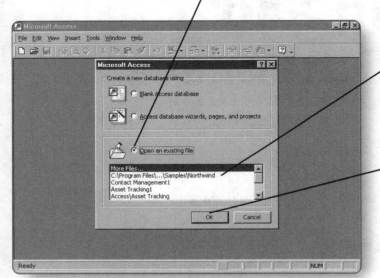

TIP

Access displays the last five databases you opened. Double-click on one to open it automatically.

2. Click on **OK**. The Open dialog box will appear.

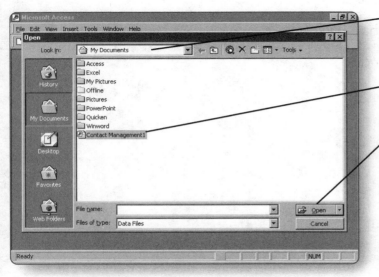

3. Click on the **folder** that contains the database you want to open.

4. Click on the **database file name** you want to open.

5. Click on the **Open button**. The database will appear in the Access window.

NOTE

You can open several existing sample databases included with Access to get ideas on how to create your own. To install them, insert the installation CD and click on the Add or Remove Features button in the Microsoft Office 2000 Maintenance Mode dialog box that displays. Change any or all of the Sample databases listed under the Microsoft Access for Windows option to run from your computer and then click on the Update Now button.

Understanding the Database Window

The left side of the Access database window includes seven buttons, each corresponding to one of the seven objects that make up an Access database. A database is essentially a collection of information. In an Access database, you collect information in tables, enter information into these tables by using forms, query tables to analyze their content, create reports based on the tables and queries, and design data access pages to view your Access data from the Web. As an advanced user, you may create macros to automate tasks or modules to create database applications using Access.

Using the Database Window

After you open a database, you can open or create tables, queries, forms, reports, and pages.

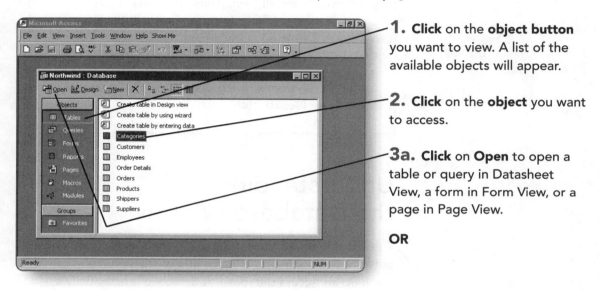

1. **Click** on the **object button** you want to view. A list of the available objects will appear.

2. **Click** on the **object** you want to access.

3a. **Click** on **Open** to open a table or query in Datasheet View, a form in Form View, or a page in Page View.

OR

3b. **Click** on **Preview** to view a report.

OR

3c. **Click** on **Design** to display the object in Design View.

OR

3d. **Click** on **New** to create a new database object. The New dialog box will open.

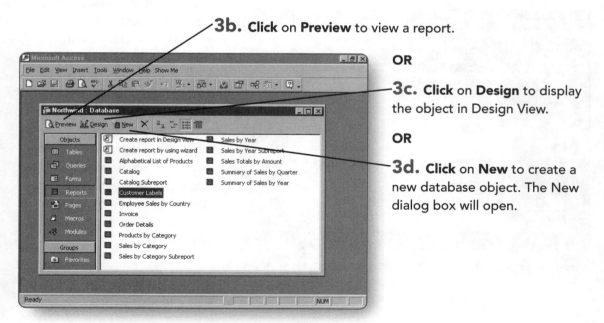

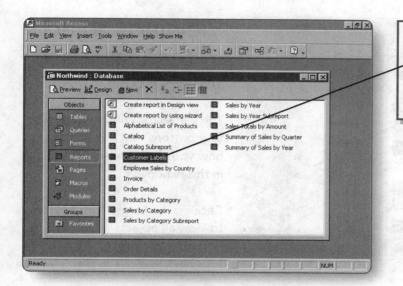

TIP

You can double-click on any object to open or preview it.

Deleting an Object in the Database Window

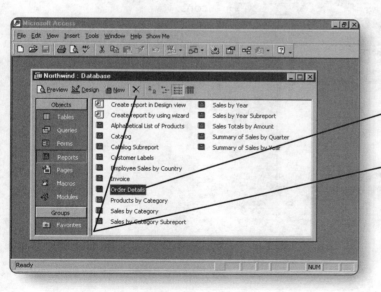

You can delete an object that you created by mistake or that you no longer need from within the Database Window.

1. Click on the **object** you want to delete.

2. Click on the **Delete button** in the database toolbar.

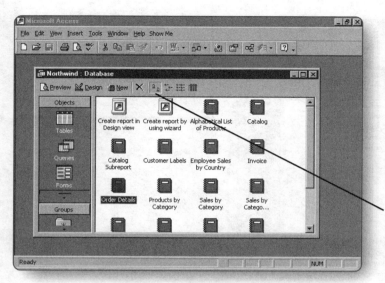

Viewing Objects in the Database Window

The Database Window includes four buttons that determine how you view available objects in this window.

Click on the Large Icons button to view all objects as large icons.

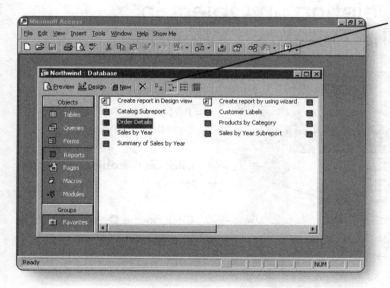

Click on the Small Icons button to view all objects as small icons.

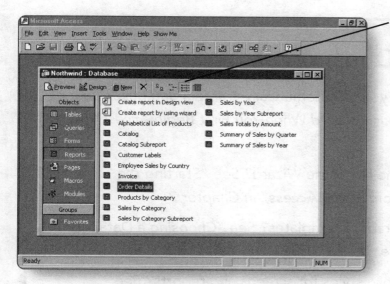

Click on the List button to view all objects as a list. This is the default viewing option.

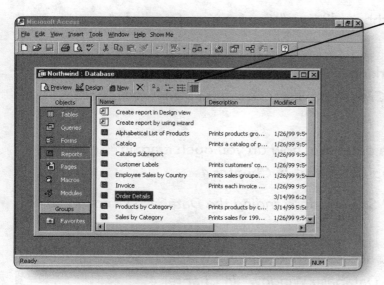

Click on the Details button to view a list of details next to each object. This list provides a description of the object, the date you last modified it, the date you created it, and the type of object it is.

Part II Review Questions

1. Which wizard helps you to automatically create a database? *See "Starting the Database Wizard When You First Begin Access" in Chapter 3*

2. How do you start the Database Wizard? *See "Starting the Database Wizard from within Access" in Chapter 3*

3. How do you use database templates? *See "Choosing a Database Template" in Chapter 3*

4. Where can you choose styles for screens and reports? *See "Customizing the Database" in Chapter 3*

5. What is a main switchboard? *See "Viewing Your Database" in Chapter 3*

6. If you're already working in Access, how do you create a database from scratch? *See "Creating a Blank Database from within Access" in Chapter 3*

7. After you've saved a database, how do you open it again? *See "Opening an Existing Database" in Chapter 4*

8. What is a database? *See "Understanding the Database Window" in Chapter 4*

9. What object can you access in the database window? *See "Understanding the Database Window" in Chapter 4*

10. What are three things you can do in the database window? *See "Using the Database Window" in Chapter 4*

PART III

Working with Tables

5

Creating a Table with the Table Wizard

The Access Table Wizard offers an easy way to create your own tables. Access includes numerous table templates that you can use to create both business and personal database tables. Access also provides step-by-step guidance as you create your database. In this chapter, you'll learn how to:

- Start the Table Wizard
- Choose table fields
- Name the table and set a key
- Set table relationships
- Finish the table

Starting the Table Wizard

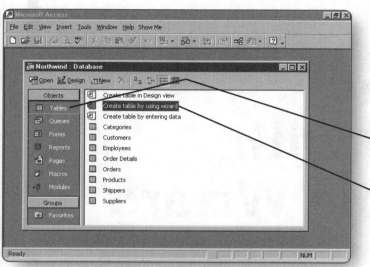

The Table Wizard can help you create common types of tables, including those that store mailing lists, recipes, investments, video collections, invoices, or exercise logs.

1. **Click** on the **Tables button** in the main database window.

2. **Double-click** on the **Create table by using wizard option**. The Table Wizard will appear.

Choosing Table Fields

Next, you choose the specific fields for your table. You can easily modify the sample tables by selecting only certain fields or by renaming the fields to something that's more appropriate for your needs.

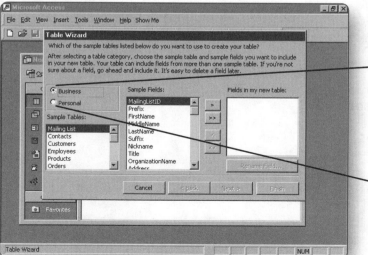

1a. **Click** on the **Business option button**. Sample business tables will appear in the Sample Tables scroll box.

OR

1b. **Click** on the **Personal option button**. Sample personal tables will appear in the Sample Tables scroll box.

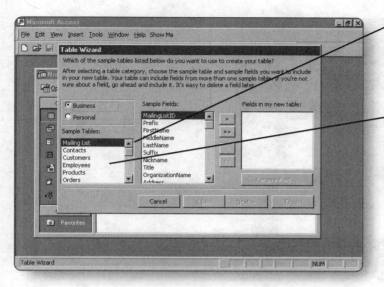

2. Scroll down the Sample Tables scroll box until you see the sample table you want to use.

3. Click on this **sample table**. Sample fields, based on the table you choose, will appear in the Sample Fields scroll box.

4. Click on the **sample field** from the Sample Fields scroll box that you want to include in your table. The field will be selected.

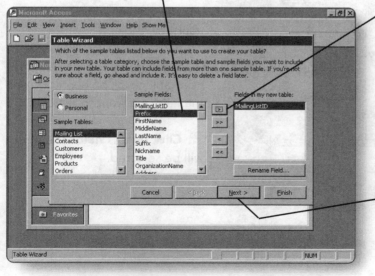

5. Click on the **right arrow button**. The sample field will move to the Fields in my new table scroll box.

6. Repeat steps 3, **4**, and **5** until you've selected all the sample fields you want to include in your table.

7. Click on **Next**. The Table Wizard will continue to the next step.

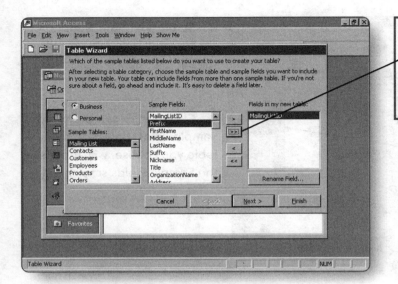

TIP

Click on the double right arrow to include all sample fields in your table.

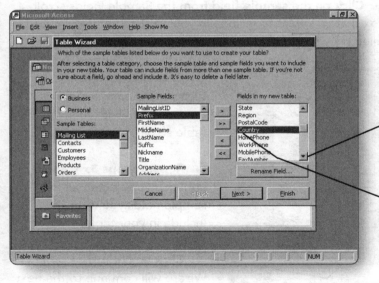

Removing Fields

You can easily remove fields that you have selected to include in your new table.

1. Scroll down the Fields in my new table scroll box until you see the field you want to remove.

2. Click on this **field.** The field will be selected.

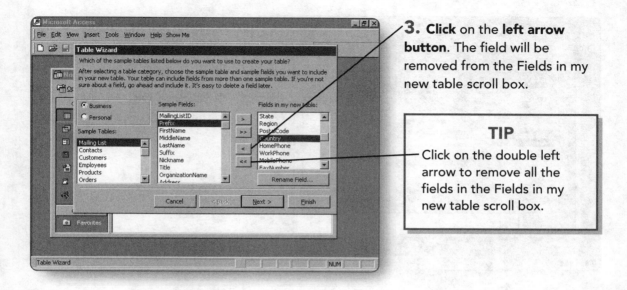

3. Click on the **left arrow button**. The field will be removed from the Fields in my new table scroll box.

Renaming Fields

You can rename a field after you move it to the Fields in my new table scroll box.

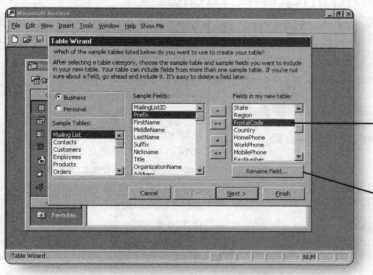

1. Click on the **field** you want to rename in the Fields in my new table scroll box.

2. Click on **Rename Field**. The Rename Field dialog box will open.

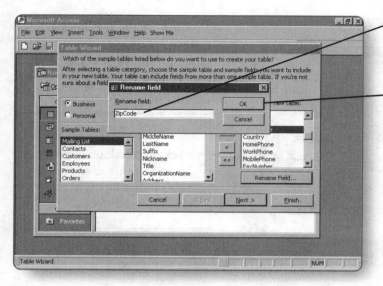

3. Enter the **new name** for the field in the Rename field text box.

4. Click on **OK**. You will return to the Table Wizard.

Naming the Table and Setting a Key

In this step of the Table Wizard, you name your table and determine how to set a primary key. A primary key is an important concept in relational database design. This key provides a unique tag for each row in your table, called a record. Access uses this primary key to relate the records in this table to another table in your database.

1. Enter a **name** for your table in the text box.

TIP

A table name can have up to 64 characters including letters, numbers, and spaces. Creating meaningful names for all parts of your database—tables, reports, forms, and queries—will help make it easier to use and manage.

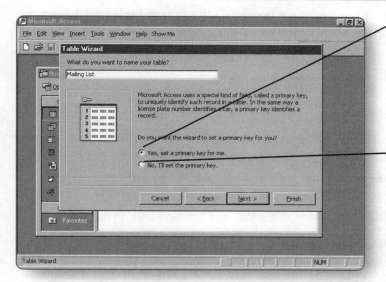

2. Click on the **Yes, set a primary key for me option button.** A primary key will automatically be set.

NOTE

The easiest way to set a primary key is to let Access set it for you. If you want to set your own key, click on the No, I'll set the primary key option button. The Table Wizard opens a new dialog box in which you can choose how to set the primary key yourself.

3. Click on **Next** to continue to the next step.

TIP

Click on the Back button to return to the previous wizard step.

Setting Table Relationships

In a relational database, you will want to relate the data from one table to another. For example, you might have a master Customers table and another table for individual Orders. You'll enter each customer once in the Customers table, but enter the customer many times in the Orders table as he or she places multiple orders. Each of these tables will have a field to identify the customer, and it is this field that relates the tables to each other.

CAUTION
You will see this step only if your database already contains at least one table. If this is the first table you are creating, you will skip this step.

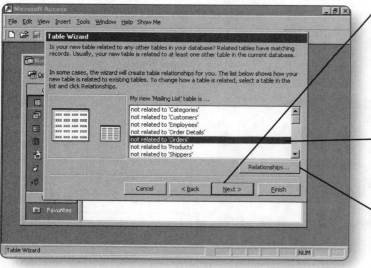

Click on Next if your new table isn't related to any existing tables. If you want to relate your new table to an existing one, Access can create the relationship for you.

1. **Click** on the **name of the existing table** you want to relate to your new table.

2. **Click** on **Relationships**. The Relationships dialog box will open.

3a. **Click** on the **One record in the 'Mailing List' table will match many records in the 'Orders' table option button**.

OR

3b. **Click** on the **One record in the 'Orders' table will match many records in the 'Mailing List' table option button**.

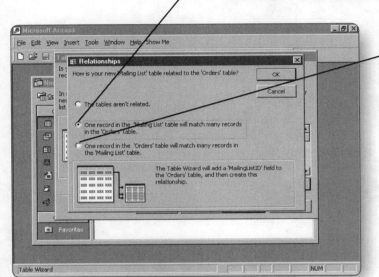

NOTE

The one-to-many distinction is very important in setting table relationships. Remember that the "one record" table should be the one with unique values for that field. For example, you would list each customer once in a Customers table and many times in an Orders table.

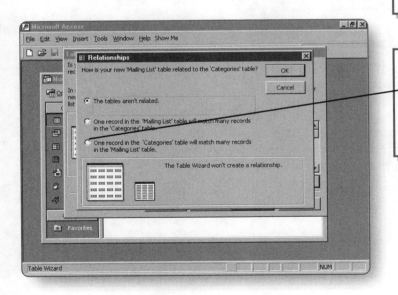

TIP

Click on The tables aren't related option button to undo a table relationship you previously made.

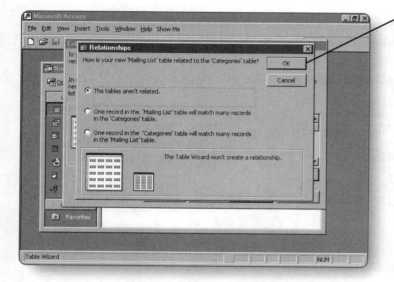

4. Click on **OK**. You will return to the Table Wizard.

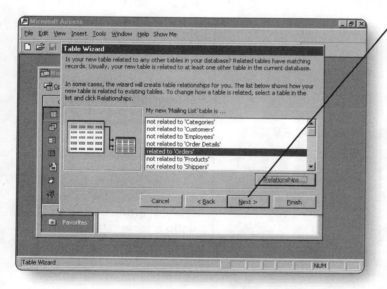

5. Click on **Next**. You will continue to the next step.

Finishing the Table

In the last step of the Table Wizard, you determine how you want to view your completed table.

1a. Click on the **Modify the table design option button**. The table will open in Design View.

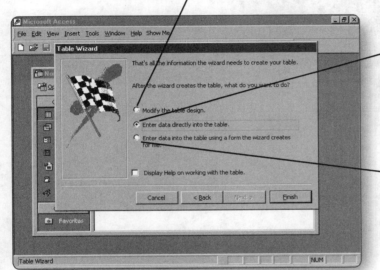

OR

1b. Click on **the Enter data directly into the table option button**. The table will open in Datasheet View.

OR

1c. Click on the **Enter data into the table using a form the wizard creates for me option button**. A form for entering data into your table will open.

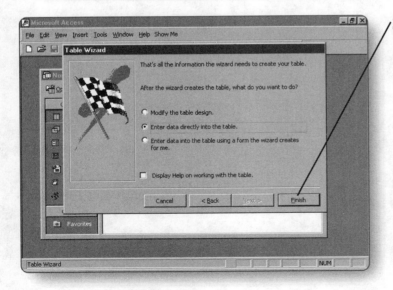

2. Click on **Finish**.

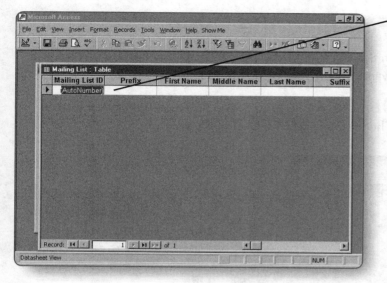

The table will open based on your instructions in step 1.

6

Creating a Table from Scratch

If you want more control over table creation than the Table Wizard provides, or if you just want to try creating a table from scratch, Access offers two different ways to do so. In this chapter, you will learn how to:

- Create a table in Datasheet View
- Create a table in Design View

Creating a Table in Datasheet View

If you want to create your own table without using the Table Wizard, you can create one in Datasheet View, then let Access analyze it and automatically set data types and a primary key. A primary key is a field that is unique in each record of your table.

When you save a table you've created in Datasheet View, Access automatically inserts an ID AutoNumber field and sets it as the primary key if, when saving, you specified that you want it to do so. Data types are set based on the type of entries you make in each column. For example, a column with currency entries will have a Currency data type. A column with only numeric entries will have a Number data type. And one with only text entries, or a mixture of text and numbers, will have a Text data type.

Even though Access automatically sets data types and the primary key when you create a table in Datasheet View, you'll still probably want to modify the field names. By default the fields are labeled Field1, Field2, etc., which isn't very descriptive or useful.

When choosing field names for your table, keep in mind that Access field names are restricted to 64 or fewer characters. You can include:

- Letters of the alphabet

- Numbers

- Special characters, except for a period, exclamation point, accent grave, or brackets

- Spaces, but only if you're not planning to use the field name in an expression or Visual Basic, both of which are advanced features of Access

1. Click on the **Tables button** in the main database window.

2. Click on **New**. The New Table dialog box will open.

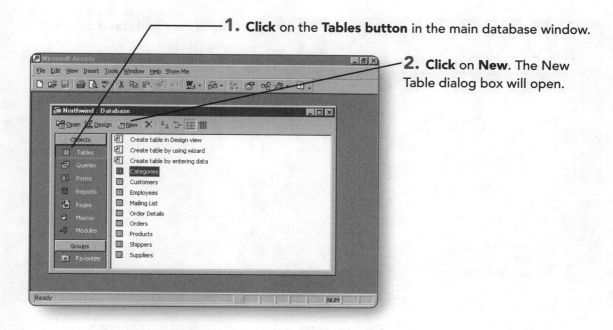

3. Click on the **Datasheet View option**.

4. Click on **OK**. A blank table will open in Datasheet View.

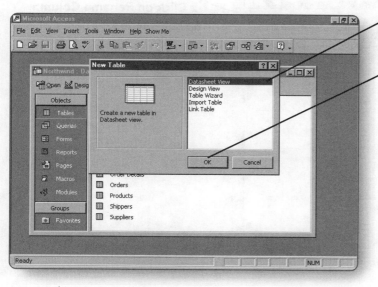

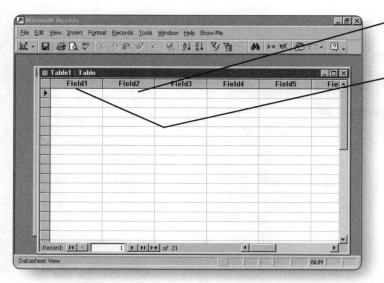

5. Enter the **desired data** into your table.

6. Click on the **column header** of the first column you want to rename.

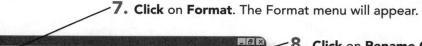

7. Click on **Format**. The Format menu will appear.

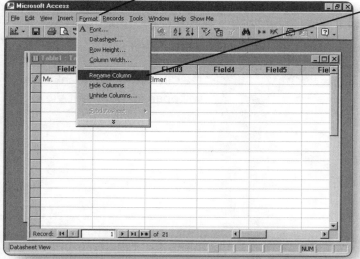

8. Click on **Rename Column**. The column header name will be selected.

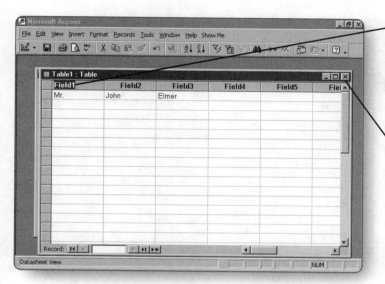

9. Type in a **new column name**.

10. Repeat steps 6 through **9** until you have renamed all necessary columns.

11. Click on the **Close button**. A dialog box will open, asking you if you want to save your new table.

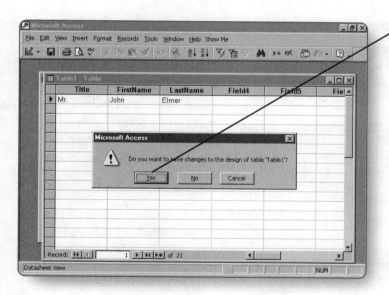

12. Click on **Yes**. The Save As dialog box will open.

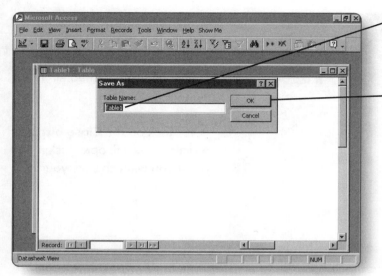

13. **Enter** the **name of your table** in the Table Name text box.

14. **Click** on **OK**. A dialog box will open, asking if you want to create a primary key.

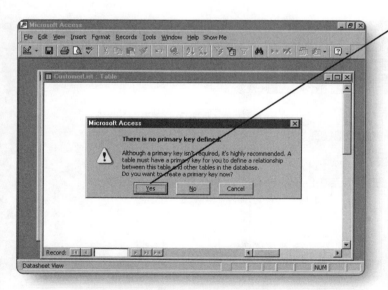

15. **Click** on **Yes**. The main database window will appear. You can now open your new table in Design View to look at the automatic defaults and make any additional modifications, such as changing a data type or adding a description.

TIP

By default, a table you create in Datasheet View includes 10 fields. If you don't need all ten, you can delete unnecessary fields by selecting them and choosing Edit, Delete Column.

Creating a Table in Design View

To gain even greater control over how you create your table, you can create it in Design View. In Design View, you enter your own field names and descriptions and choose your own data type to associate with each field. You can also set your own primary key.

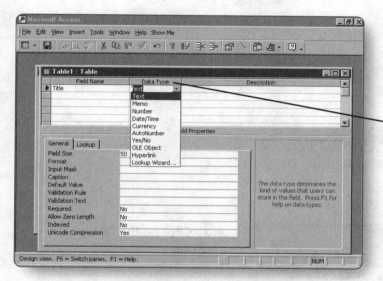

Before creating a table entirely from scratch, you should write down your basic table structure on paper, focusing particularly on field names and data types.

Access fields can have one of the following data types:

- **Text**. Stores text or combinations of text and numbers—such as addresses—up to 255 characters.

- **Memo**. Stores text and numbers up to 64,000 characters; used for detailed, descriptive fields.

- **Number**. Stores numeric data that you can use in calculations.

- **Date/Time**. Stores a field in date or time format.

- **Currency**. Stores currency data that you can use in calculations.

- **AutoNumber**. Stores a sequential number for each record.

- **Yes/No**. Stores only one of two values such as Yes/No, True/False, or On/Off.

- **OLE Object**. Stores objects created in another application—such as Word or Excel—that you can link to or embed in an Access table.

- **Hyperlink**. Stores a link to a Web page, e-mail address, or another object in the database.

- **Lookup Wizard**. Stores a lookup column that you can reference from another table.

1. Click on the **Tables button** in the main database window.

2. Click on **New**. The New Table dialog box will open.

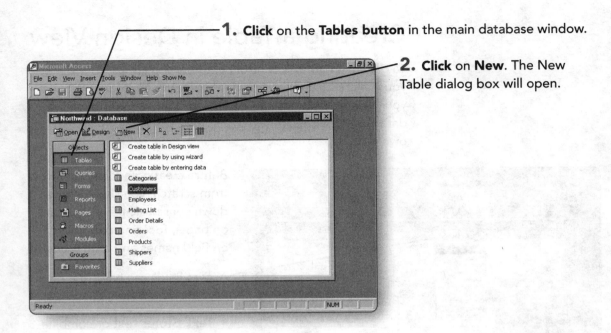

3. Click on the **Design View option**.

4. Click on **OK**. A blank table will open in Design View.

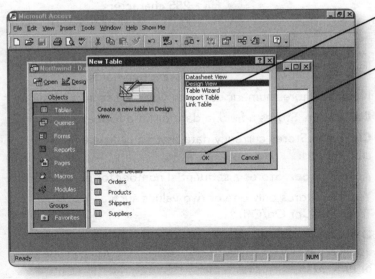

5. Enter the **first field name** in the Field Name column.

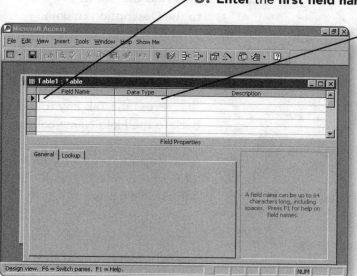

6. Press the **Tab key** to move to the Data Type column.

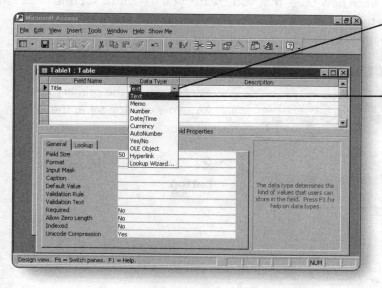

7. Click on the **down arrow** to the right of the field. A list of available data types will appear.

8. Click on the **desired data type**.

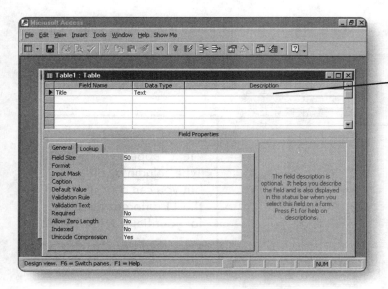

9. **Press** the **Tab key** to move to the Description column.

10. **Enter** a **description** of this field. Doing so is optional.

11. **Press** the **Tab key** to move back to the Field Name column.

12. **Repeat steps 5** through **11** until you have finished entering fields.

Setting a Primary Key

In each new table that you create, you'll want to set one field as the primary key. Access uses this key to relate this table's records to those in another table.

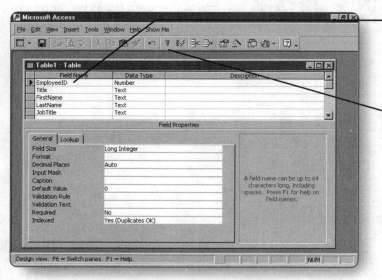

1. **Click** on the **field** that you want to set as the primary key. An arrow will appear in the field selector column.

2. **Click** on the **Primary Key button**.

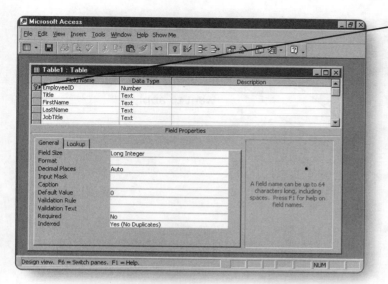

The field will be set as the primary key, indicated by a small key in the field selector column. The primary key is a toggle. To remove it, select the primary key field and click on the Primary Key button again.

Setting Format Properties

Access always sets each field with the default format for its data type. This format defines how the field displays in tables, forms, and reports. You may want to change this format to one of the other options. For example, a field with a Currency data type has a format of Currency by default. By changing the format, however, you can display this field in other ways, such as a percentage.

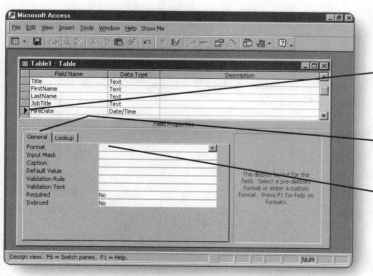

1. Click on the **field** whose format properties you want to set.

2. Click on the **General tab** in the Field Properties area.

3. Click on the **Format text box**. A down arrow will appear.

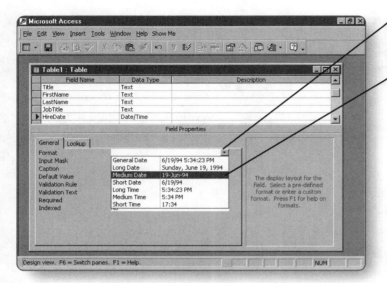

4. Click on the **down arrow** to display a list of possible formats.

5. Click on the **format** you want to apply.

Setting Field Size Properties for Text Fields

The default field size for a field with a data type of Text is 50 characters. You can change this size to an amount anywhere in the range of 0 to 255 characters.

CAUTION

If you've already entered data in a table and you decrease the field size, you could lose some of your existing data if its length exceeds the new field size.

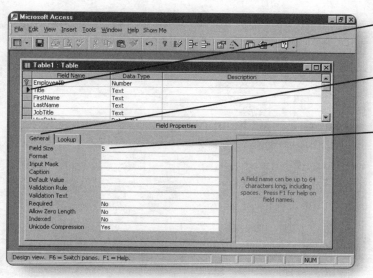

1. **Click** on the **field** whose field size you want to change.

2. **Click** on the **General tab** in the Field Properties area.

3. **Enter** the **new field size** in the Field Size text box.

Saving the Table

Once you finish creating your table, you'll want to save it.

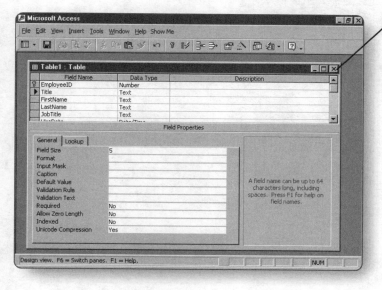

1. **Click** on the **Close button**. A dialog box will open, asking if you want to save the table.

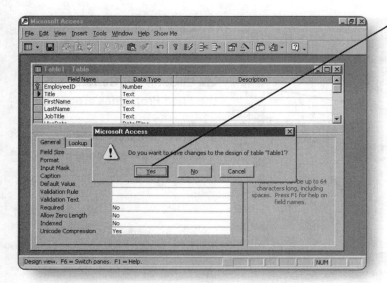

2. **Click** on **Yes**. The Save As dialog box will open.

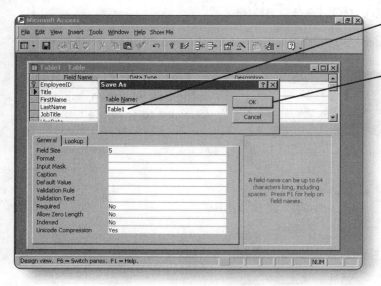

3. **Enter** a **name for your table** in the Table Name text box.

4. **Click** on **OK**. The main database window will appear again.

7

Modifying a Table

Once you create an Access table, you can easily modify it by adding, deleting, moving, or renaming table fields. In this chapter, you will learn how to:

- Open a table in Design View
- Insert, delete, rename, and move fields
- Change the data type

Opening a Table in Design View

To modify a table's design, you must open it in Design View.

1. **Click** on the **Tables button** in the main database window.

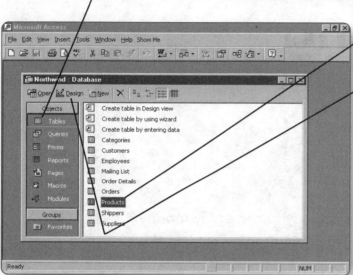

2. **Click** on the **table** you want to open. It will be highlighted.

3. **Click** on the **Design button**. The table will open in Design View.

NOTE

You can also open a table in Design View directly from the Table Wizard by choosing the Modify the table design option button in the final wizard step.

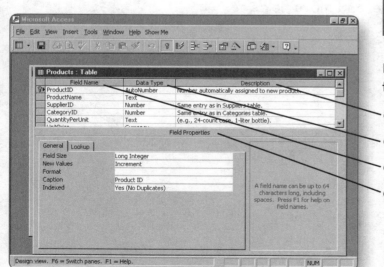

In Design View, you see each field's underlying structure:

- Description
- Data Type
- Field Name
- Field Properties

Inserting a Field

You can insert a field into an existing table.

1. Click on the **row** beneath which you want to add a field. An arrow will appear in the field selector column.

2. Click on the **Insert Rows button**.

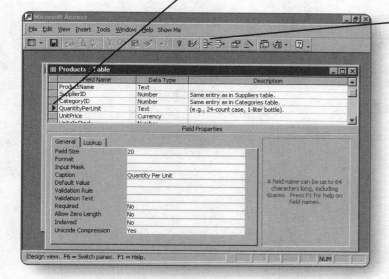

A blank row will be added.

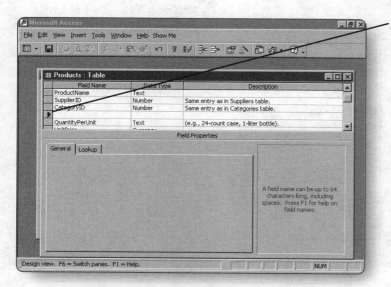

Deleting a Field

You can easily delete a field from a table.

1. Click on **the field row** that you want to delete. An arrow will appear in the field selector column.

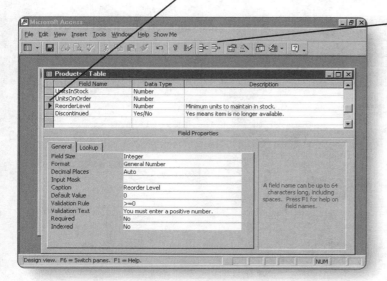

2. Click on the **Delete Rows button**. A dialog box appears asking if you want to permanently delete the field and all its data.

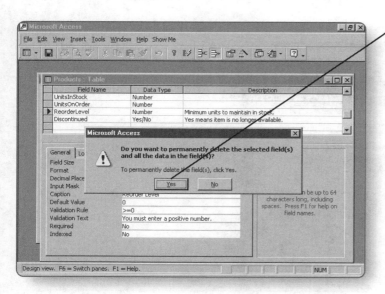

3. Click on **Yes**. The field will be permanently deleted.

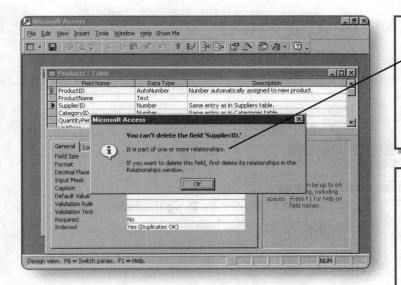

CAUTION

If you've used the field in a report, form, or query somewhere else in the database, Access tells you that you can't delete it.

TIP

To delete more than one field at a time, select the first field and, holding down the Ctrl key, continue selecting the remaining fields you want to delete.

Renaming a Field

You can also easily rename a field in an Access table. Remember that renaming a field can also affect reports, forms, and queries that contain the field. If you must rename the field in the table, you'll need to rename it in all other objects that contain it.

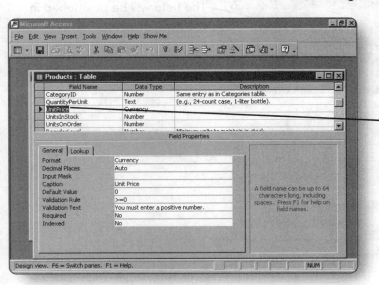

1. Select the **Field Name** that you want to rename.

2. Enter the **new name**.

Moving a Field

You can change the order of the fields in your table if you need to.

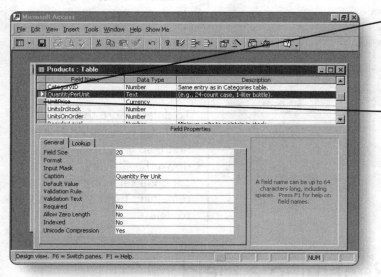

1. Click on the **field row** that you want to move. An arrow will appear in the field selector column.

2. Drag the **field** to a new location.

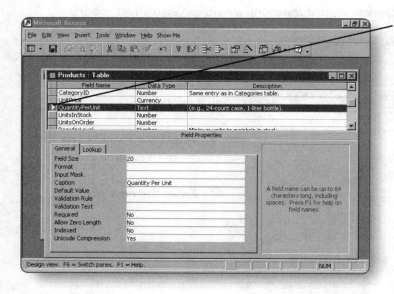

The field will be positioned in the new location.

Changing the Data Type

You can change the data type of existing table fields. For example, you might want to change a number field to a currency field.

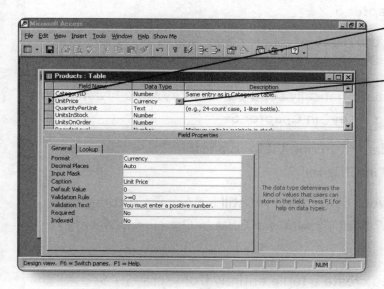

1. **Click** on the **field** whose data type you want to change.

2. **Click** on the **down arrow** to the right of the Data Type field whose data type you want to change. A menu will appear.

CAUTION

Remember that changing the data type of a field may restrict the types of entries you can make or even truncate existing entries. Also be sure that the data type you choose is compatible with the existing data. For example, if your existing field contains text and you change the data type to Numeric, Access displays a warning telling you that you will lose all of your data if you make this data type change.

---

3. **Click** on the **new data type**. The new data type will become permanent when you save the table.

Part III Review Questions

1. Which wizard automatically creates a new table? *See "Starting the Table Wizard" in Chapter 5*

2. How do you change the name of a field? *See "Renaming Fields" in Chapter 5*

3. Where does Access automatically set a primary key? *See "Naming the Table and Setting a Key" in Chapter 5*

4. How do you relate data from one table to another? *See "Setting Table Relationships" in Chapter 5*

5. How do you create your own table, yet still let Access automate certain tasks for you? *See "Creating a Table in Datasheet View" in Chapter 6*

6. In which view can you create a table entirely from scratch? *See "Creating a Table in Design View" in Chapter 6*

7. How do you set a unique key for each record in your table? *See "Setting a Primary Key" in Chapter 6*

8. In which view can you open a table to modify it? *See "Opening a Table in Design View" in Chapter 7*

9. How do you add a new field to an existing table? *See "Inserting a Field" in Chapter 7*

10. Where do you change the data type of an existing table field? *See "Changing the Data Type" in Chapter 7*

PART IV

Entering, Editing, and Viewing Data

8

Entering Data

Access offers two ways to enter data into tables. You can
enter new data while existing data is in view, or you can hide
the existing data while you enter new data. In this chapter, you
will learn how to:

- Open a table in Datasheet View
- Use Edit mode to enter data
- Use Data Entry mode to enter data

Opening a Table in Datasheet View

To enter data in a table, you need to open it in Datasheet View.

1. Click on the **Tables button** in the main database window.

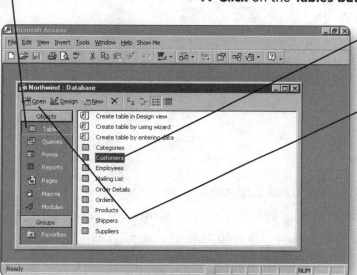

2. Click on the **table** that you want to open. It will be highlighted.

3. Click on the **Open button**. The table will open in Datasheet View.

NOTE

You can also open a table in Datasheet View directly from the Table Wizard by choosing the Enter data directly into the table option button in the final wizard step.

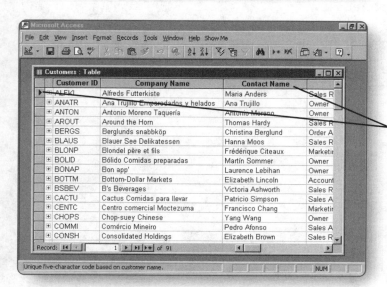

Datasheet View looks similar to a spreadsheet such as those you see in Excel 2000. It uses a row and column format to display table data in a series of fields. Each row is referred to as a *record*.

Navigating in Datasheet View

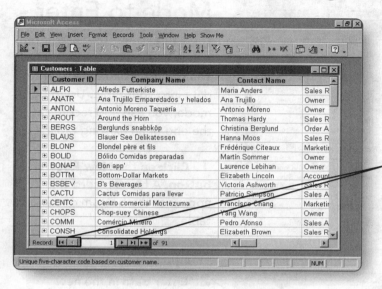

Access identifies the current record with an arrow in the record selector column. The record number box at the bottom of the screen also displays the current record number.

This box is surrounded by several navigation buttons that help you navigate the table. Using these buttons, you can move to the first, preceding, next, or last record.

You can also use the mouse to navigate the datasheet or to select the field you want. In addition, Access provides several other navigation commands. See Appendix B, "Using Keyboard Shortcuts," for a more detailed list.

Enter or Tab	Navigates to the next field.
Shift+Tab	Navigates to the preceding field.
Page Up	Navigates up one screen.
Page Down	Navigates down one screen.

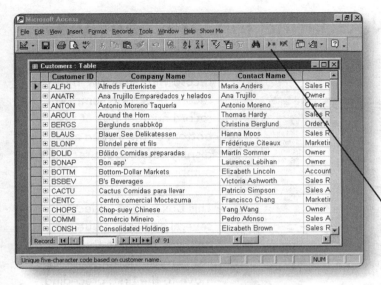

Using Edit Mode to Enter Data

You can use *Edit mode* to enter data into your table. Using Edit mode, you can add records at the end of an existing table.

1. Click on the **New Record button**. A blank record will appear at the bottom of the table.

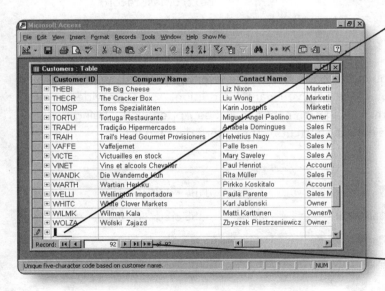

2. Enter data in the new record.

3. Tab to the **next blank record** when you finish entering data in the first.

4. Repeat steps 2 and **3** until you're finished adding data.

TIP
You can also click on the New Record button to the right of the navigation buttons to add a new record.

NOTE
Access automatically enters the next consecutive number in an AutoNumber field once you tab out of it.

Using Data Entry Mode to Enter Data

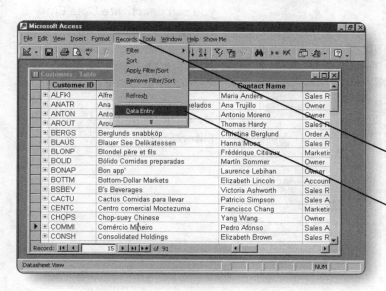

You can also use Data Entry mode to enter data into a datasheet. Data Entry mode displays a blank table and temporarily hides all previously entered records from view.

1. **Click** on **Records**. The Records menu will appear.

2. **Click** on **Data Entry**. Data Entry mode will be activated.

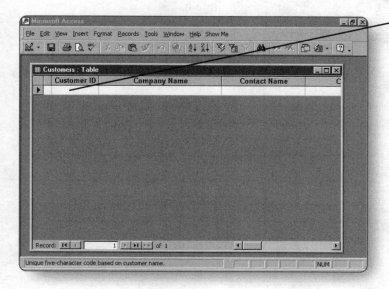

3. **Enter data** in the new record.

4. **Tab** to the **next blank record** when you finish entering data in the first.

5. **Repeat steps 3** and **4** until you finish adding data.

Exiting Data Entry Mode

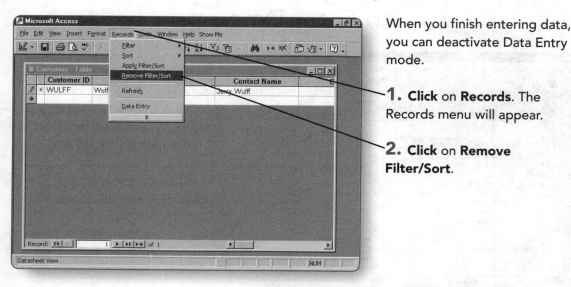

When you finish entering data, you can deactivate Data Entry mode.

1. Click on **Records**. The Records menu will appear.

2. Click on **Remove Filter/Sort**.

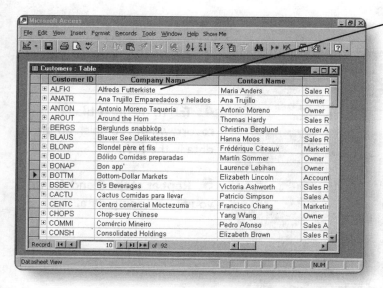

The hidden records will appear again.

9

Editing Data

You can edit and modify data in Access with the security of knowing that you can undo your last edit. Access also includes a powerful find and replace feature that lets you quickly update large amounts of data. In this chapter, you will learn how to:

- Modify data
- Undo edits
- Replace data
- Delete records

Modifying Data

You can modify an existing table entry in Datasheet View by replacing all or part of the data.

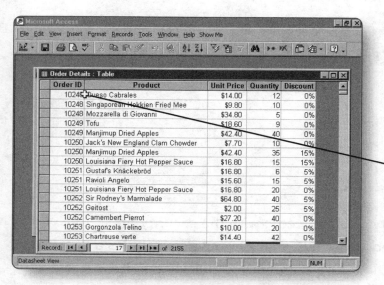

Modifying the Entire Field Contents

You can replace the entire contents of the selected field.

1. Place the **mouse pointer** on the left side of the field. A large white plus sign will appear.

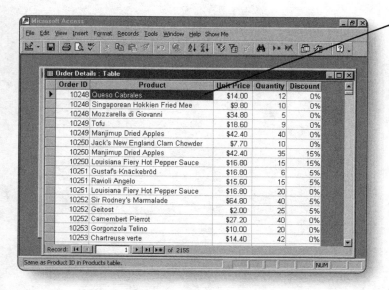

2. Click on the **field**. The entire field will be highlighted.

3. Replace the **existing field data** with new data.

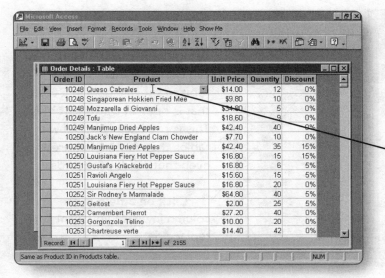

Modifying Partial Field Contents

You can replace parts—such as individual words—of selected field contents.

1. Click on the **field** whose data you want to modify. The I-beam pointer will appear.

2. Replace the **desired data** with new information.

Undoing Edits

If you make a mistake while editing data, you can often undo it. Undo lets you undo the last edit you made. Depending on your last action, the label for the Undo button may display Undo Typing, Undo Current Field/Record, or Undo Saved Record. If there is nothing to undo, the button label will display Can't Undo.

To use the Undo feature, click on the Undo button on the toolbar. The last edit will be undone.

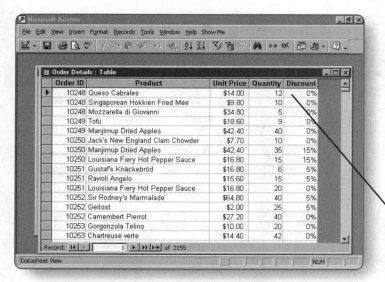

Replacing Data

Using the Replace feature, you can quickly search for and replace specific data in a table that is open in Datasheet View. This is particularly useful with tables that contain hundreds or even thousands of records.

1. Click on a **field** in the column in which you want to replace data.

2. Click on **Edit**. The Edit menu will appear.

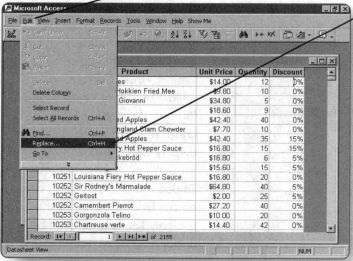

3. Click on **Replace**. The Find and Replace dialog box will open with the Replace tab selected.

TIP

If the Replace menu option doesn't appear, click on the double down arrows at the bottom of the Edit menu. Additional menu options will be displayed.

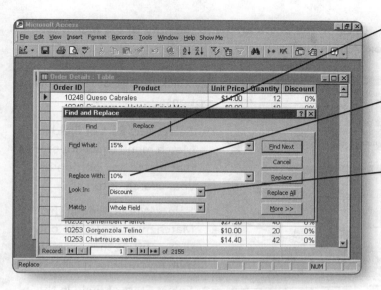

4. **Enter** the **text** that you want to replace in the Find What text box.

5. **Enter** the **text** that you want use as a replacement in the Replace With text box.

6 **Click** on the **down arrow** to the right of the Look in: list box. A menu will appear.

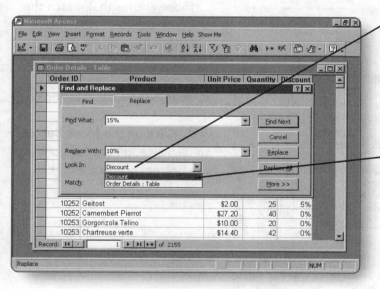

7a. **Click on** the **default field name** in order to search only the field you selected in step 1. The default field name will appear in the Look in list box.

OR

7b. **Select** the **table name** to replace fields throughout the entire table.

8. Click on the **down arrow** to the right of the Match list box. A menu will appear.

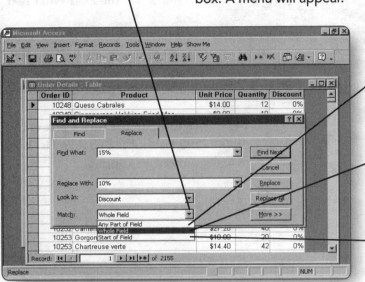

9. Click on one of the following options:

- Select Any Part of Field in the Match menu to locate entries that match any portion of your search criteria.

- Select Whole Field in the Match menu to locate only those entries that exactly match your search criteria.

- Select Start of Field in the Match menu to locate only those entries that match the initial letters of your search criteria.

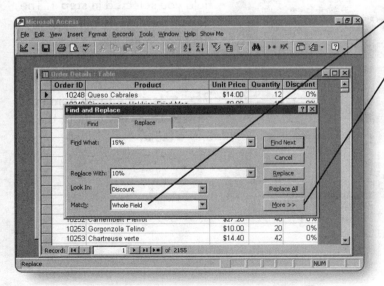

The option you select will appear in the Match: list box.

10. Click on the **More button** to display additional options at the bottom of this dialog box.

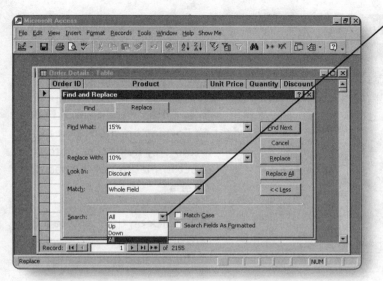

11. Click on the **down arrow** to the right of the Search list box. A menu will appear.

12. Click on one of the following **options**:

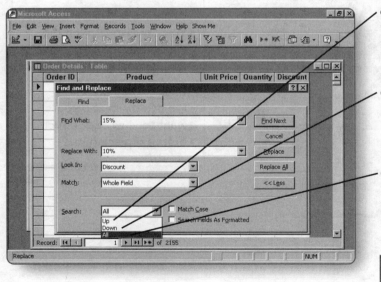

- Choose Up from the Search drop-down list to search only the records prior to the currently selected record.

- Choose Down from the Search drop-down list to search only the records after the currently selected record.

- Choose All from the Search drop-down list to search the entire table for your specified criteria.

NOTE

The record in which you clicked to select the search field in step 1 is the currently selected record.

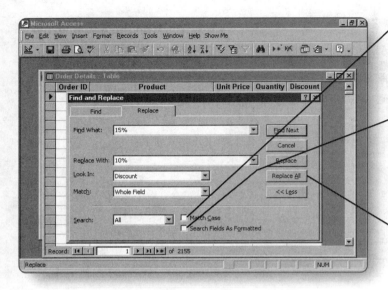

13. Click on the **Match Case check box** to locate only those entries that exactly match the case in your search criteria.

14. Click on the **Search Fields As Formatted check box** to locate only fields that match the exact formatting of the search criteria.

15. Click on the **Replace All button** to replace all instances of the entered text.

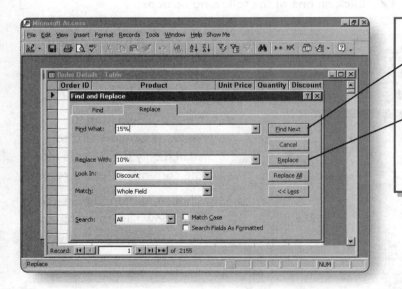

TIP

You can also click on the Find Next button to find the next match.

Click on Replace to replace the text if you want to view each match before replacing it.

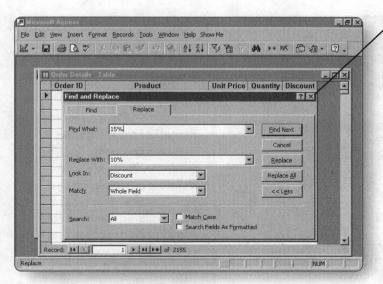

16. **Click** on **Close** to exit the Find and Replace dialog box.

Deleting Records

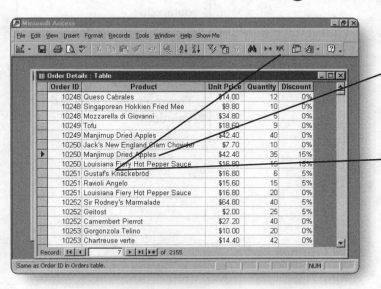

You can delete records from Access tables.

1. **Click** on the **record selector column** of the record you want to delete. An arrow will appear in the column.

2. **Click** on the **Delete Record button**. A warning message box will appear.

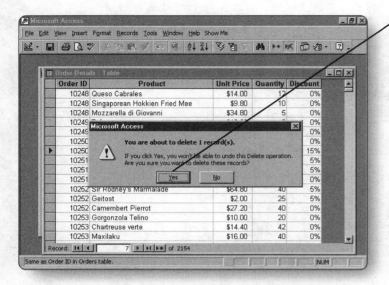

3. Click on **Yes** to permanently delete the record.

CAUTION

You can't delete a record if another table includes it in related records. For example, if you try to delete a customer record in a Customers database and a related Orders table includes an order for that customer, you won't be able to delete that customer record. Access displays a dialog box that informs you if the record you selected can't be deleted.

NOTE

You can't undo a record deletion.

10

Sorting, Filtering, and Finding Data

Access includes several features that help you locate, organize, and analyze specific information in your tables while in Datasheet View. In this chapter, you'll learn how to:

- Sort data
- Filter data
- Find data

Sorting Data

With a table open in Datasheet View, you can sort data in one or more fields in either ascending or descending order.

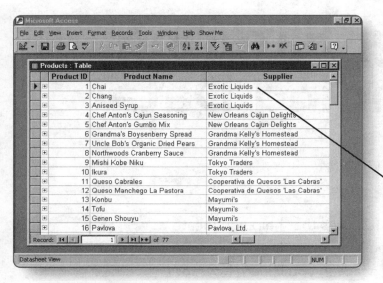

TIP

Remember that to open a table in Datasheet View, you can double-click on the table name in the main database window.

1. Click on the **field or fields** on which you want to sort.

TIP

To sort more than one field, click on the first field, then press and hold the Shift key as you click on additional fields.

2a. Click on the **Sort Ascending button** in the toolbar.

OR

2b. Click on the **Sort Descending button** in the toolbar.

NOTE

If you select more than one field on which to sort, Access will sort the fields in order from left to right.

Removing a Sort

After applying a sort, you can remove it and restore the default order of the table data.

1. Click on **Records**. The Records menu will appear.

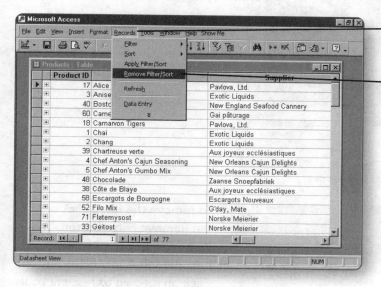

2. Click on **Remove Filter/Sort**. The default order of the table data will be restored.

Filtering Data

Filter by Selection lets you select specific data in a table that is open in Datasheet View, then quickly apply a basic filter. For example, if you want to view only records for customers located in San Francisco, you could click on any field containing the words "San Francisco" and apply Filter by Selection to view these records.

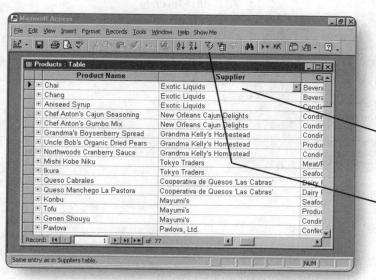

1. Click on a **field** that contains the data on which you want to filter.

2. Click on the **Filter by Selection button**.

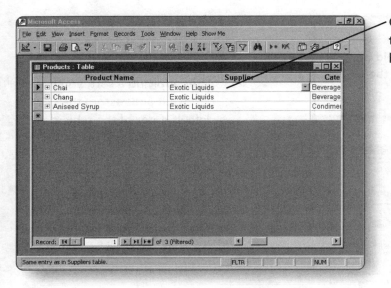

Only the records that contain this data are displayed. Access hides all other records.

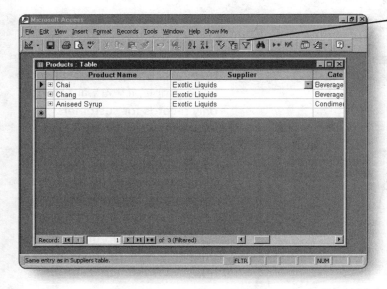

To remove the filter, click on the Remove Filter button. The Remove Filter button will become the Apply Filter button. Click on it again to reapply your last filter.

Filtering by Form

The Filter by Form feature lets you filter based on more than one criterion. Using this feature, you can filter based on both AND and OR criteria. If you specify AND criteria, Access will display only those records that meet all the specified criteria. For example, if you filter on both customers located in San Francisco and customers in the real estate industry, only records with both criteria will be displayed. If you filter on customers in San Francisco or customers in the real estate industry, then records that meet either condition will be displayed.

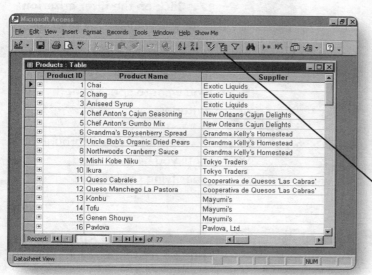

1. **Click** on the **Filter by Form button**. The Filter by Form window will appear with the Look For tab active.

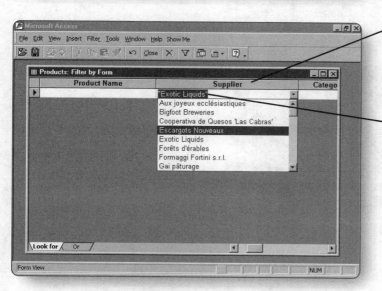

2. **Click** on the **field** on which you want to filter. A down arrow and menu will appear to the right of the selected field.

3. **Click on** the **filter criterion** that you want to use from the menu.

4. **Repeat steps 2** and **3** until you have selected all desired AND criteria.

5. Click on the **Or tab** if you want to specify OR criteria.

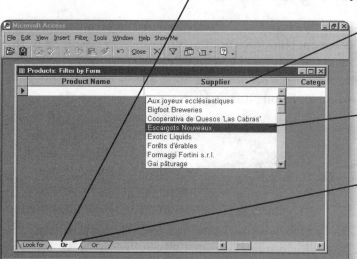

6. Click on the **field** on which you want to filter. A down arrow and menu will appear to the right of the selected field.

7. Click on the **filter criterion** that you want to use from the drop-down list.

8. Click on the **next Or tab** if you want to specify another OR criterion.

9. Repeat steps 6 through **8** until you have finished specifying OR criteria.

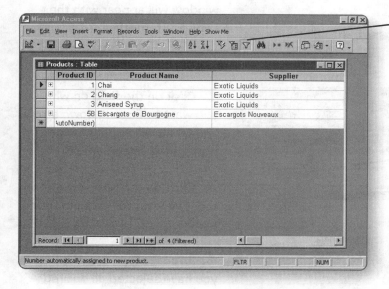

10. Click on the **Apply Filter button**. The filter results will appear.

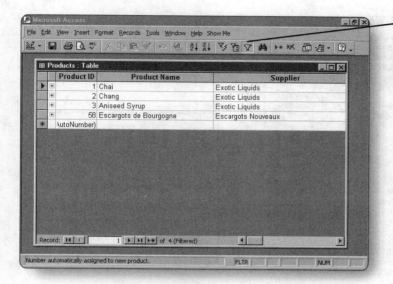

Once you've viewed the filter results, click on the Remove Filter button to remove the filter and restore the original data.

Saving a Filter by Form

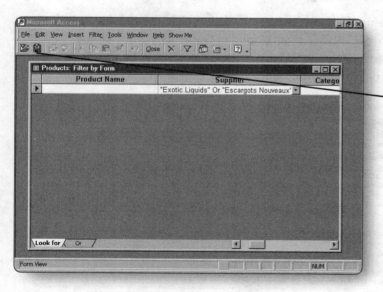

While you are in the Filter by Form window, you can save filter by form results as a query.

1. Click on the **Save As Query button**. The Save As Query dialog box will open.

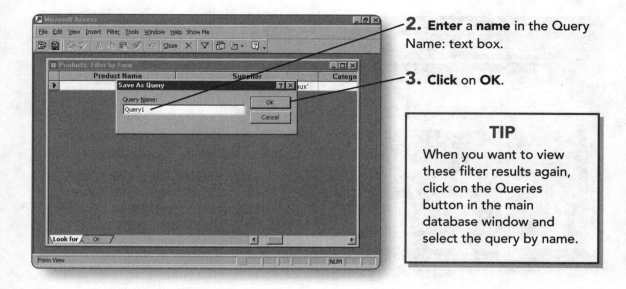

2. Enter a **name** in the Query Name: text box.

3. Click on **OK**.

TIP

When you want to view these filter results again, click on the Queries button in the main database window and select the query by name.

Finding Data

Using the Find feature, you can quickly search for specific data in a table that is open in Datasheet View. This is particularly useful with tables that contain hundreds or even thousands of records.

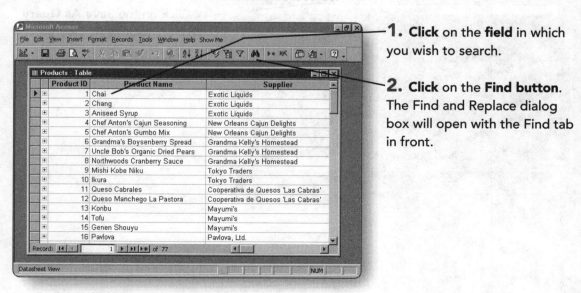

1. Click on the **field** in which you wish to search.

2. Click on the **Find button**. The Find and Replace dialog box will open with the Find tab in front.

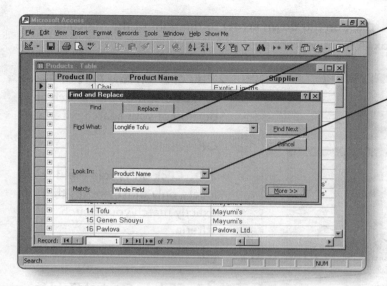

3. Enter the **word or words** on which you want to search in the Find What text box.

4. Click on the **down arrow** to the right of the Look In list box. A menu will appear.

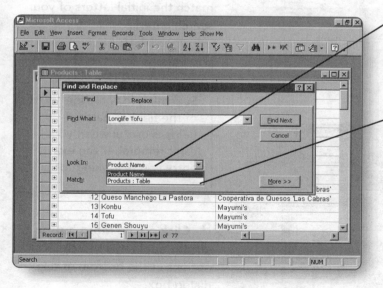

5a. Click on the **default field name** in order to search only the field you selected in step 1.

OR

5b. Click on the **table name** to search the entire table.

6. Click on the **down arrow** to the right of the Match list box. A menu will appear.

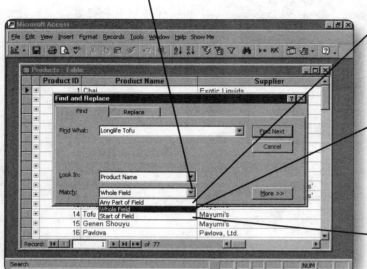

7a. Click on **Any Part of Field** to locate entries that match any portion of your search criteria.

OR

7b. Click on **Whole Field** to locate only those entries that exactly match your search criteria.

OR

7c. Click on **Start of Field** to locate only those entries that match the initial letters of your search criteria.

TIP

Searching for only the start of the field or parts of fields is useful when you can't remember the exact entry you're looking for.

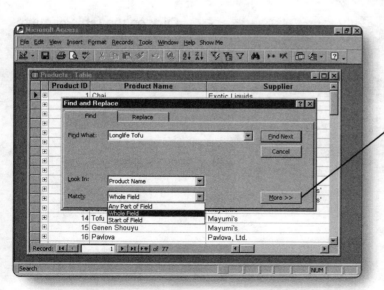

8. Click on the **More button** to display additional search options at the bottom of this dialog box.

9. Click on the **down arrow** to the right of the Search list box. A menu will appear.

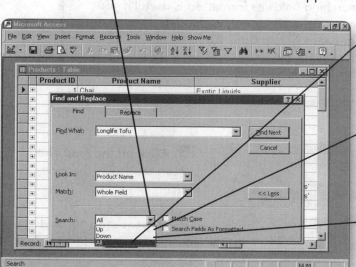

10a. Click on **All** to search the entire table for your specified criteria.

OR

10b. Click on **Up** to search only the records prior to the currently selected record.

OR

10c. Click on **Down** to search only the records after the currently selected record.

NOTE

The currently selected record is the record in which you clicked to select the search field in step 1.

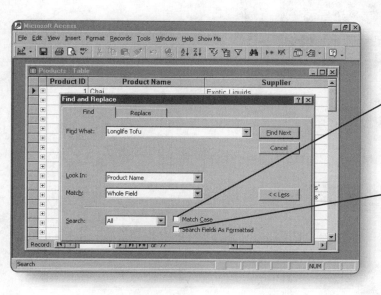

11. Click on the **Match Case check box** to locate only those entries that exactly match the case in your search criteria.

12. Click on the **Search Fields As Formatted check box** to locate only fields that match the exact formatting of the search criteria.

NOTE

Searching fields as formatted is useful if you want to search for only exact date formatting. For example, entering 10/15/00 would not match with the entry October 15, 2000 if this check box is selected.

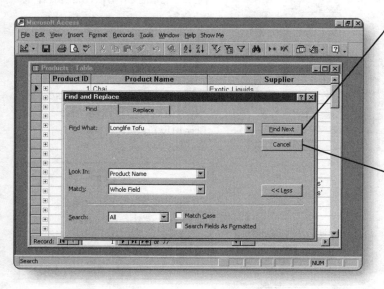

13. **Click** on the **Find Next button** to display the next match.

14. **Repeat step 13** until you've viewed all desired matches.

15. **Click** on **Cancel** to exit the Find and Replace dialog box.

11

Revising the Datasheet Layout

In Datasheet View, you can make many layout modifications to display the datasheet in the format that's most convenient for you. In this chapter, you'll learn how to:

- Resize datasheet columns and rows
- Freeze and unfreeze columns
- Hide and unhide columns
- Rename columns
- View subdatasheets

Resizing Datasheet Columns

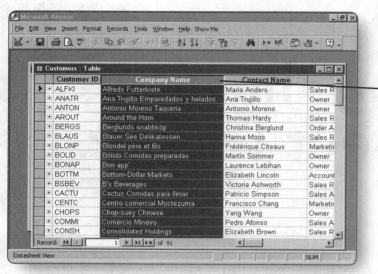

In Datasheet View, you can resize the width of individual columns.

1. Click on the **column indicator button** of the column you want to resize. It will be highlighted.

2. Click on **Format**. The Format menu will appear.

3. Click on **Column Width**. The Column Width dialog box will open.

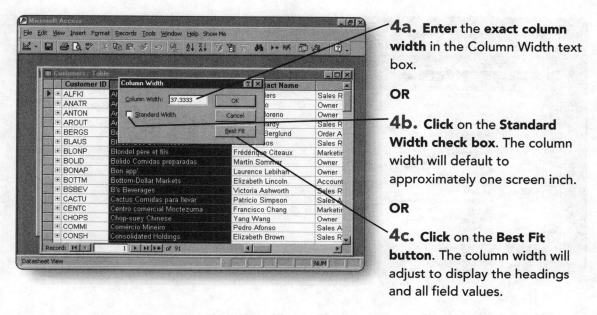

4a. Enter the **exact column width** in the Column Width text box.

OR

4b. Click on the **Standard Width check box**. The column width will default to approximately one screen inch.

OR

4c. Click on the **Best Fit button**. The column width will adjust to display the headings and all field values.

5. Click on **OK** if the dialog box didn't automatically close when you clicked on the Best Fit button.

TIP

You can also automatically set the best fit by double-clicking the black arrow that appears when you place the mouse pointer to the right of a column header.

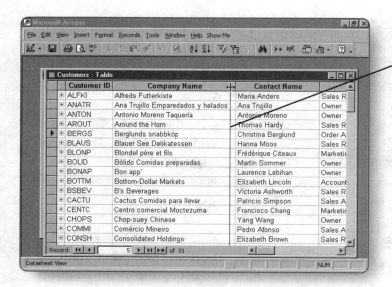

TIP

To manually adjust the column width, drag the black arrow to the left or right to reposition the column grid.

Resizing Datasheet Rows

You can resize row height in Datasheet View.

1. Click on **Format**. The Format menu will appear.

2. Click on **Row Height**. The Row Height dialog box will open.

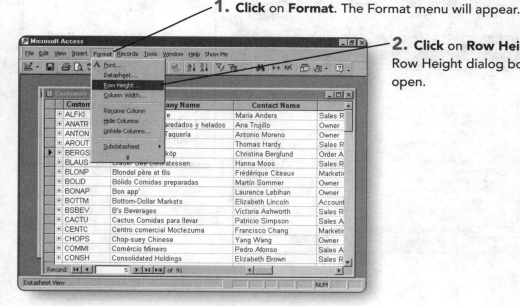

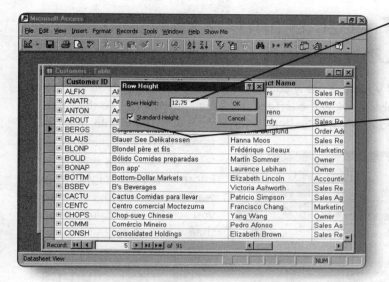

3a. Enter the **exact row height** in the Row Height text box.

OR

3b. Click on the **Standard Height check box**. The row height will default to approximately 12.75 points.

4. Click on **OK**.

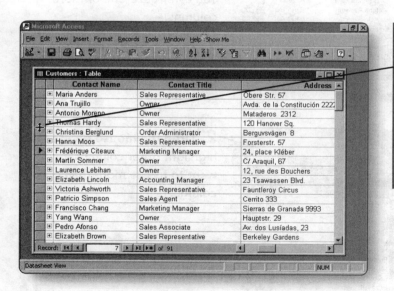

TIP

To manually adjust the row height, place the mouse pointer next to the record locator column; when it turns into an up-down arrow, resize the row as desired.

Freezing and Unfreezing Columns

If you have many columns (fields) in your table, you won't be able to view the left-most columns if you scroll to the right. If you want a column or columns to always be visible, you can freeze them. For example, in a table that contains employee information, you might always want to see employee names as you scroll across columns to view their information.

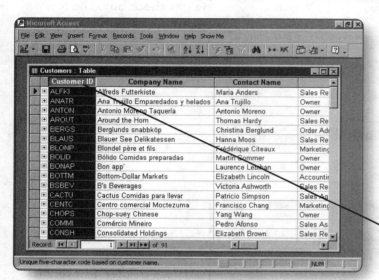

Freezing Columns

You can freeze one or more columns.

1. Click on the **column header** of the first column you want to freeze.

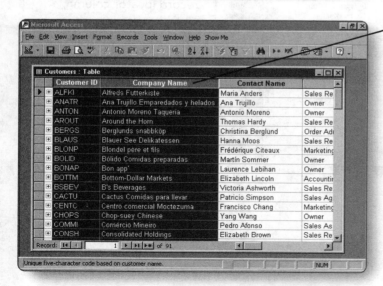

2. Drag the **mouse pointer** to highlight other columns if you want to freeze more than one column.

3. Click on **Format**. The Format menu will appear.

4. Click on **Freeze Columns**.

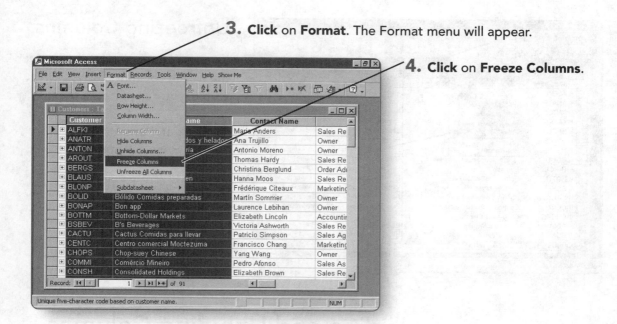

A black line will appear in the grid to the right of the last frozen column.

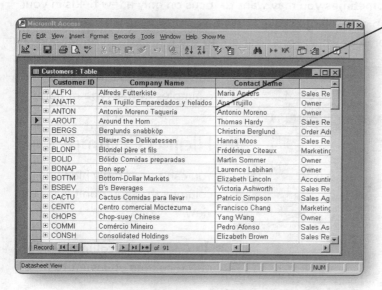

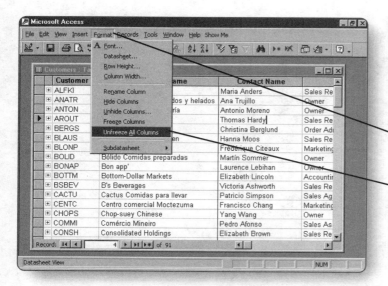

Unfreezing Columns

If you no longer want to have the frozen columns always visible, you can unfreeze them.

1. Click on **Format**. The Format menu will appear.

2. Click on **Unfreeze All Columns**.

Hiding and Unhiding Columns

Sometimes you may want to focus on only a few fields in your table. In a large table, it can be confusing to view many fields, some of which are important to the table structure but convey no necessary information. ID and AutoNumber fields are examples of this type of field.

Hiding Columns

You can temporarily hide any columns that you don't want to view.

1. Click on the **column header** of the column you want to hide.

2. Drag the **mouse pointer** to include other columns if you want to hide more than one column.

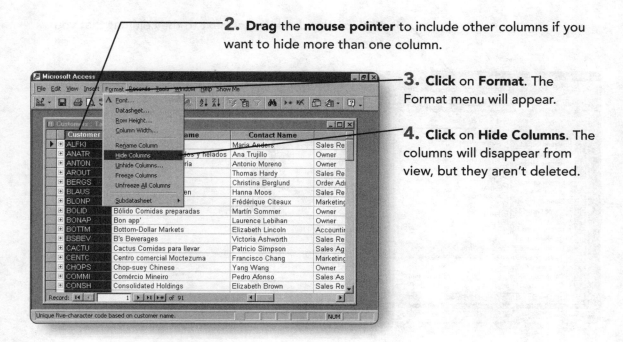

3. Click on **Format**. The Format menu will appear.

4. Click on **Hide Columns**. The columns will disappear from view, but they aren't deleted.

Unhiding Columns

You'll use the Unhide Columns dialog box to select the columns you want to unhide. A check mark appears in the check boxes of all visible columns; hidden columns have no check mark.

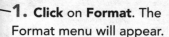
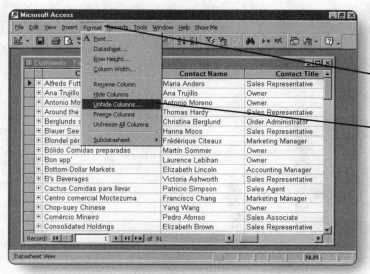

1. Click on **Format**. The Format menu will appear.

2. Click on **Unhide Columns**. The Unhide Columns dialog box will open.

3. Click on the **check boxes** next to the columns that you want to unhide.

4. Click on **Close**. The columns will appear again.

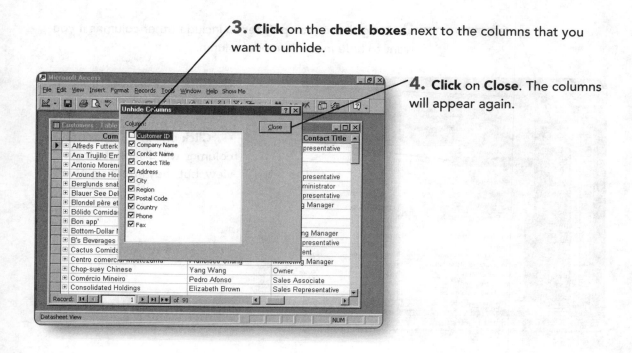

Renaming Columns

You can rename a field column directly in Datasheet View.

1. Click on the **column header** of the column that you want to rename.

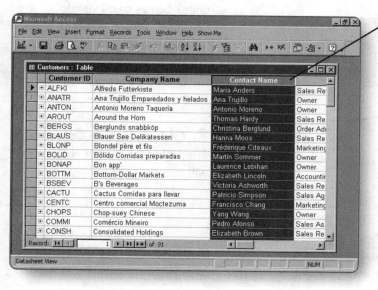

2. Click on **Format**. The Format menu will appear.

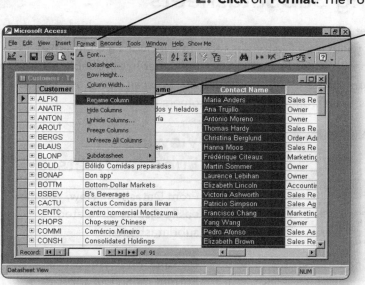

3. Click on **Rename Column**. The column header name will be selected.

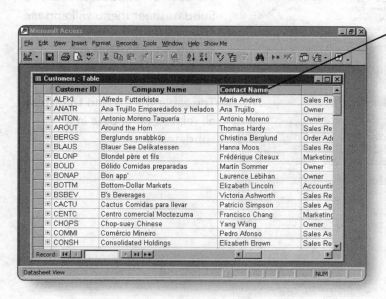

4. Type in a **new column name** and **press Enter**. When you save the table, the new column (field) name will be permanent.

NOTE

You can't rename more than one column at a time.

Viewing Subdatasheets

In Datasheet View you can view the data of other related tables. For example, if you have a Customers table that includes a one-to-many relationship with an Orders table, each customer has probably placed more than one order. Using subdatasheets, you can view a list of orders for each customer from within the Customers table.

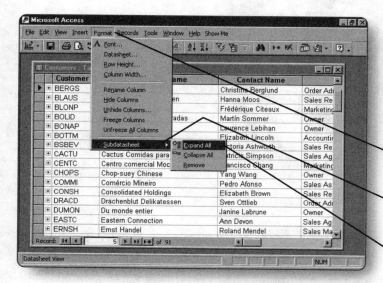

Viewing All Subdatasheets

From Datasheet View, you can easily display all related subdatasheets.

1. **Click** on **Format**. The Format menu will appear.

2. **Click** on **Subdatasheet**. The Subdatasheet menu will appear.

3. **Click** on **Expand All**.

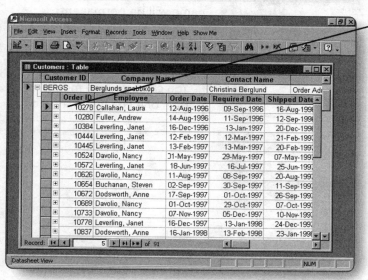

The table will expand to display all related table data in a subdatasheet.

Closing Subdatasheets

You can collapse the subdatasheet when you're finished viewing it.

1. Click on **Format**. The Format menu will appear.

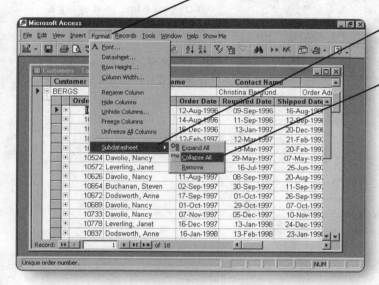

2. Click on **Subdatasheet**. The Subdatasheet menu will appear.

3. Click on **Collapse All**.

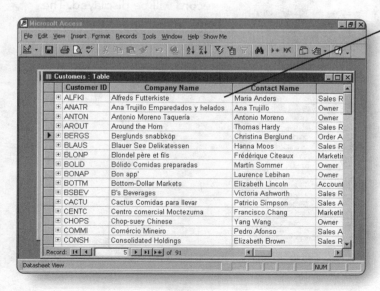

The table will return to normal Datasheet View.

Viewing a Single Subdatasheet

You can view a subdatasheet for an individual record (row) rather than for the entire table.

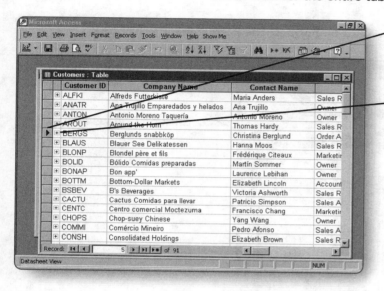

1. **Click on** the **record** for which you want to display a subdatasheet.

2. **Click** on the **plus sign** at the far left of the highlighted record.

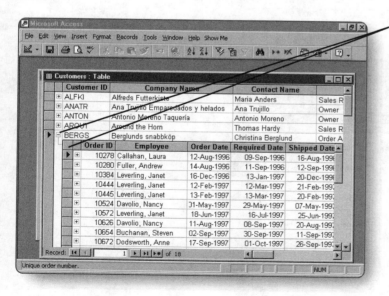

A subdatasheet for that table record will be displayed. The plus sign changes to a minus sign.

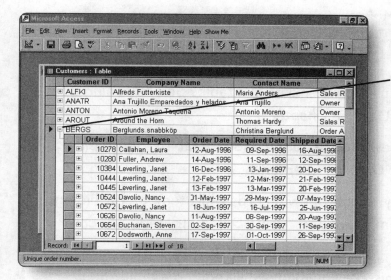

Collapsing a Single Subdatasheet

To collapse a single subdatasheet, click on the minus sign to the left of the record. The original Datasheet View will be restored.

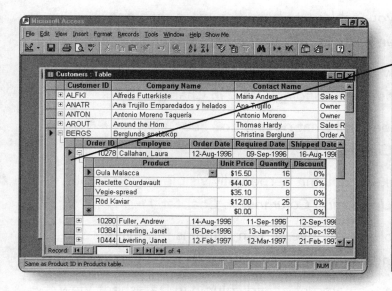

NOTE

You can continue expanding subdatasheets if they are available. For example, if you display a subdatasheet for a particular row, the subdatasheet displays a plus sign to the left of every record that also contains related table data. Click on this plus sign to expand another level of subdatasheet.

Part IV Review Questions

1. Which view do you use to enter data in a table? *See "Opening a Table in Datasheet View" in Chapter 8*

2. How can you add new records to the end of a table? *See "Using Edit Mode to Enter Data" in Chapter 8*

3. What's the best way to enter new records while temporarily hiding existing records from view? *See "Using Data Entry Mode to Enter Data" in Chapter 8*

4. Want to correct a mistake you made while editing a table? *See "Undoing Edits" in Chapter 9*

5. How can you filter your table data based on more than one criterion? *See "Filtering by Form" in Chapter 10*

6. How can you quickly find a specific word in a table that contains thousands of records? *See "Finding Data" in Chapter 10*

7. What's a subdatasheet and what does it do? *See "Viewing Subdatasheets" in Chapter 11*

8. What command makes a column perpetually visible as you scroll? *See "Freezing and Unfreezing Columns" in Chapter 11*

9. How can you temporarily remove certain columns from view? *See "Hiding and Unhiding Columns" in Chapter 11*

10. How do you change the name of a field column in Datasheet View? *See "Renaming Columns" in Chapter 11*

PART V

Creating and Using Forms

12

Creating an AutoForm

The simplest and easiest way to create a form is to use the AutoForm feature. Using AutoForm, you can automatically create columnar, tabular, and datasheet forms based on a table or query you select. In this chapter, you'll learn how to:

- Create a Columnar AutoForm
- Create a Tabular AutoForm
- Create a Datasheet AutoForm
- Save and close a form

Creating a Columnar AutoForm

You can automatically create a columnar form based on a selected table or query using the AutoForm feature. In a columnar form, one record will appear onscreen at a time, in a vertical format.

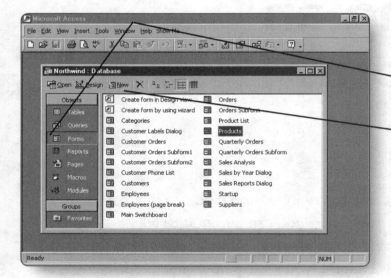

1. Click on the **Forms button** in the main database window.

2. Click on **New**. The New Form dialog box will open.

3. Click on the **AutoForm: Columnar** option.

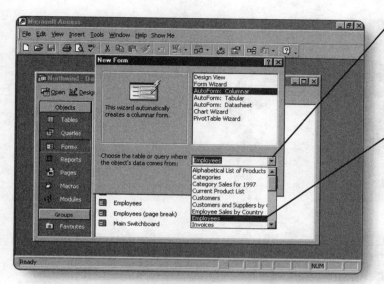

4. Click on the **down arrow** next to the Choose the table or query where the object's data comes from list box. A menu will appear.

5. Click on the **desired table**.

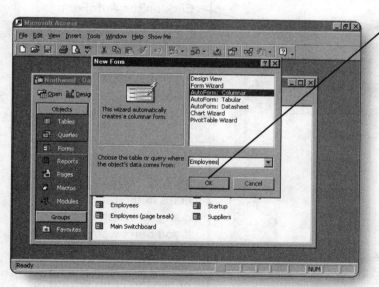

6. Click on **OK**.

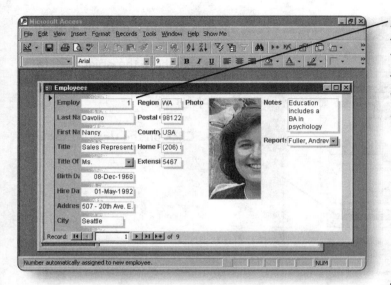

A columnar form based on this table will appear in Form View. You can begin entering data in the form immediately if you want. Or, you can modify its appearance to suit your needs.

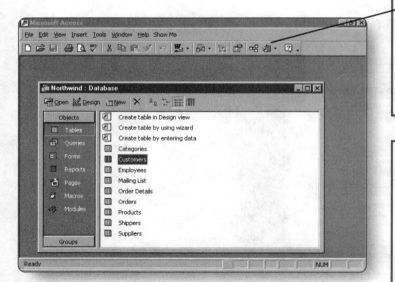

TIP

Click on the AutoForm button on the toolbar to quickly create a columnar AutoForm based on the current open or selected table.

NOTE

An AutoForm includes all fields in the table or query on which it's based. If you don't want these defaults, you can later modify the form's design or use the Form Wizard to create your own form instead.

Creating a Tabular AutoForm

You can also automatically create a tabular form based on a selected table or query. The tabular form displays your table data in rows and columns.

1. Click on the **Forms button** in the main database window.

2. Click on **New**. The New Form dialog box will open.

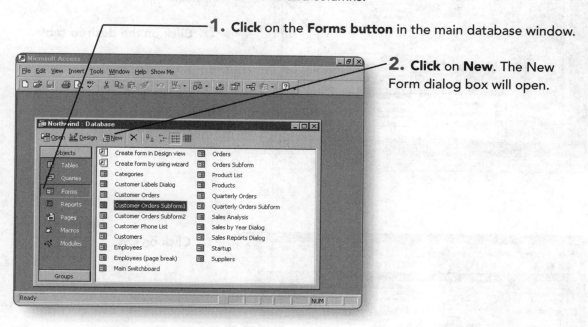

3. Click on the **AutoForm: Tabular** option.

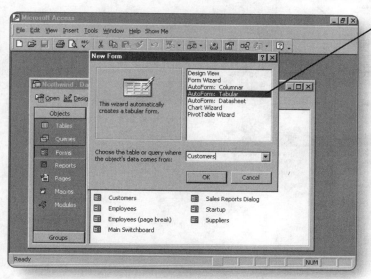

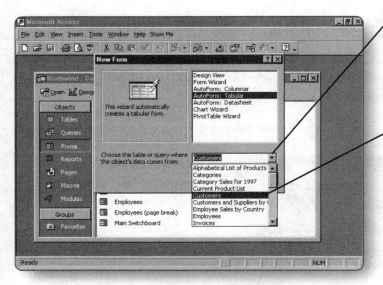

4. Click on the **down arrow** next to the Choose the table or query where the object's data comes from list box. A menu will appear.

5. Click on the **desired table**.

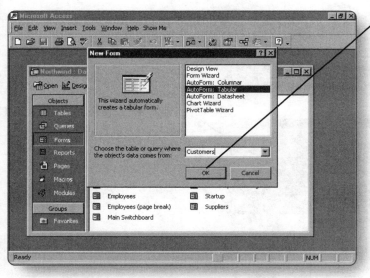

6. Click on **OK**.

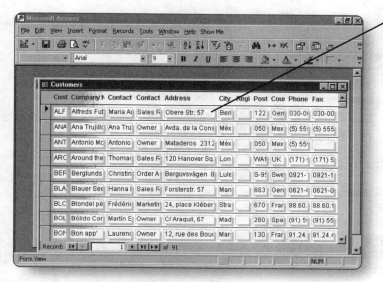

A tabular form based on this table will appear in Form View.

Creating a Datasheet AutoForm

The third AutoForm option is the Datasheet AutoForm. This type of form displays your data in the familiar Datasheet View.

1. Click on the **Forms button** in the main database window.

2. Click on **New**. The New Form dialog box will open.

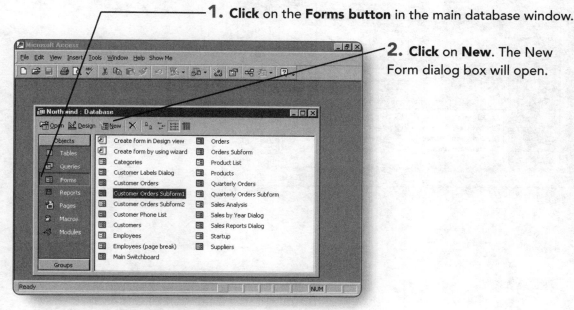

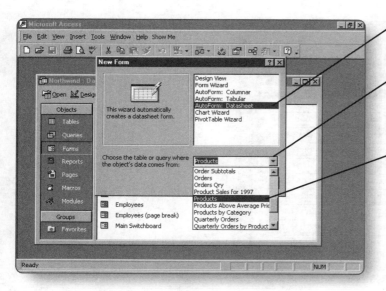

3. Click on the **AutoForm: Datasheet** option.

4. Click on the **down arrow** to the right of the list box. A menu will appear.

5. Click on the **desired table**.

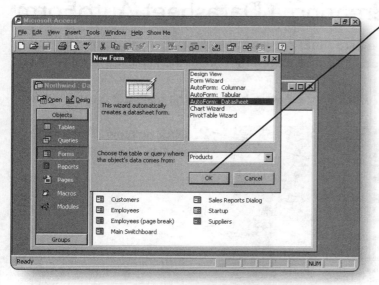

6. Click on **OK**.

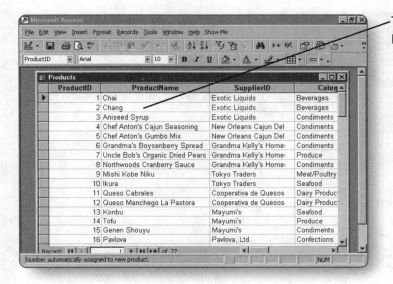

The form will appear in Datasheet View.

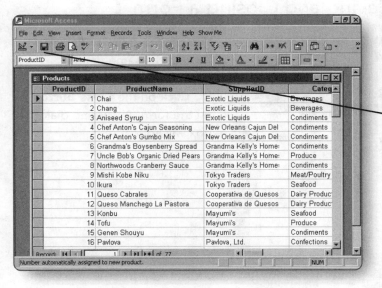

Saving a Form

Once you create a form, you'll want to save it.

1. Click on the **Save button**. The Save As dialog box will open.

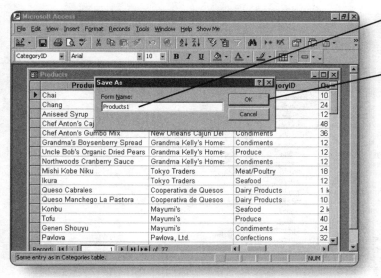

2. Enter a **name** for your form in the Form Name text box.

3. Click on **OK**. The form will be saved, but will remain open.

Saving and Closing a Form

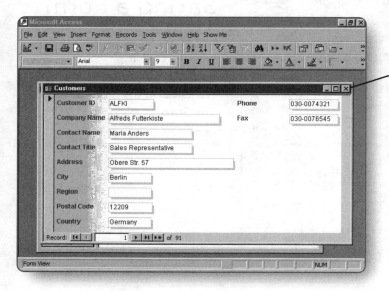

You can also save and close a form at the same time.

1. Click on the **Close button** on the form. A warning dialog box will appear.

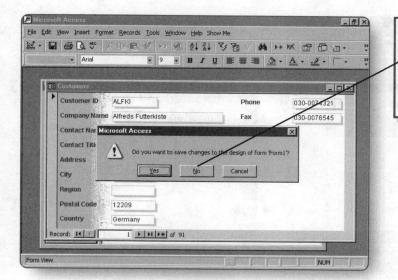

TIP
Click on No in the warning dialog box to close and discard the form.

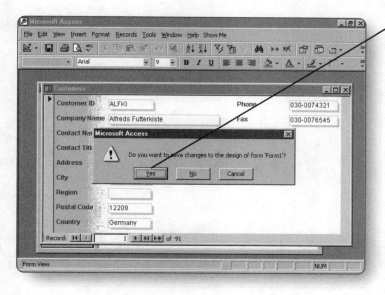

2. Click on **Yes** to save the form. The Save As dialog box will open.

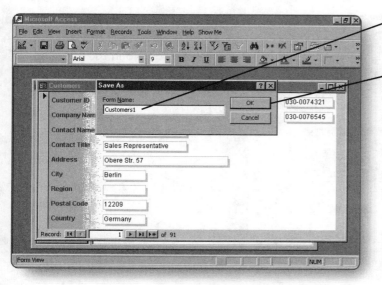

3. Enter a **name** for your form in the Form Name text box.

4. Click on **OK**. The form will be saved and closed simultaneously.

13

Creating a Form with the Form Wizard

The Access Form Wizard helps you build a basic form while offering step-by-step guidance. Using the wizard, you can quickly create a basic form by specifying the fields you want to include, as well as the form layout and style. In this chapter, you'll learn how to:

- Start the Form Wizard
- Select fields for your form
- Choose a form layout
- Choose a form style
- Finish the form

Starting the Form Wizard

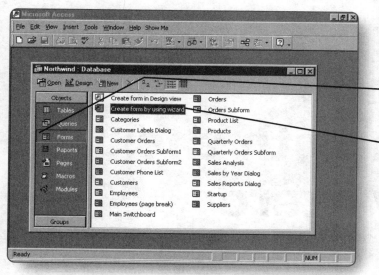

The Form Wizard can help you select the fields, layout, and style for your form.

1. **Click** on the **Forms button** in the main database window.

2. **Double-click** on **Create form by using wizard** within the window. The Form Wizard will open.

Selecting Fields for Your Form

After you open the wizard, you select specific fields to place in your form. Using the Form Wizard, you can select fields from more than one table or query.

TIP

Before creating a form, think carefully about the fields you need to include. Including all of the fields in a specific table or query will often overcrowd a form, or the fields may not all fit.

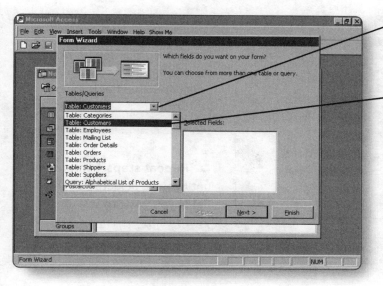

1. Click on the **down arrow** to the right of the Tables/Queries list box. A menu will appear.

2. Click on the **table or query** from which you want to select a field. A list of the fields for that table/query will appear.

3. Scroll down the **Available Fields scroll box** until you see the first field you want to include in your form.

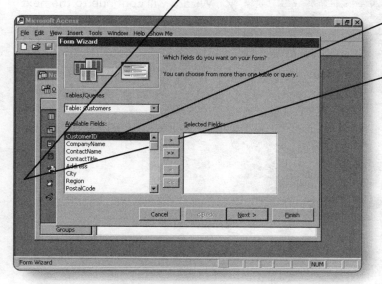

4. Click on **the field.** The field will be highlighted.

5. Click on the **right arrow button.** The field will move to the Selected Fields list.

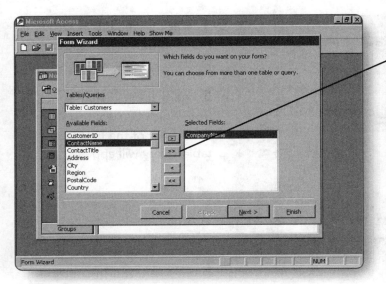

TIP
Click on the double right arrow button to include all available fields in your form.

6. Repeat steps 1 through **5** until you've selected all the fields you want to include in your form.

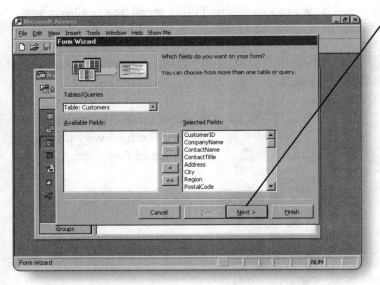

7. Click on **Next**. The Form Wizard will continue to the next step.

Choosing a Form Layout

You can choose from four different form layouts:

- **Columnar**. Each field displays on its own line preceded by a label.

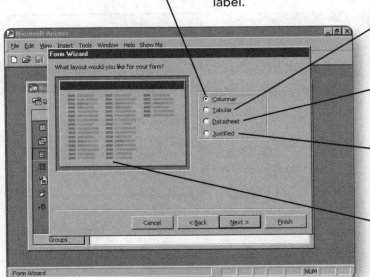

- **Tabular**. For each record, the fields display on one line with labels on the top row.

- **Datasheet**. The fields display as a table datasheet using rows and columns.

- **Justified**. The fields for each record display justified in the form.

The preview box displays a sample of what the selected layout will look like.

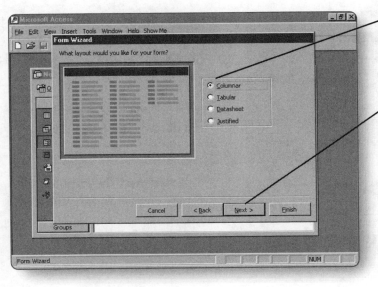

1. Click on the **form layout option button** for the format that you want to apply to your form.

2. Click on **Next** to continue.

Choosing a Form Style

Access includes several predefined form styles from which you can choose. The ten form styles range from casual to serious and include both colors and gray tones.

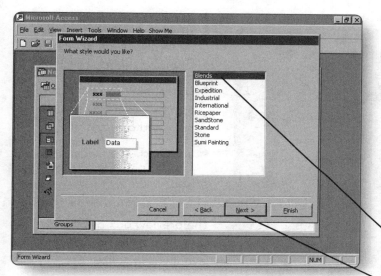

TIP

Be sure that the form style you choose is consistent with existing forms and reports in your database. Style consistency will make your database both easier to use and more pleasing to look at.

1. Click on the **form style** you want to display on your form.

2. Click on **Next** to continue.

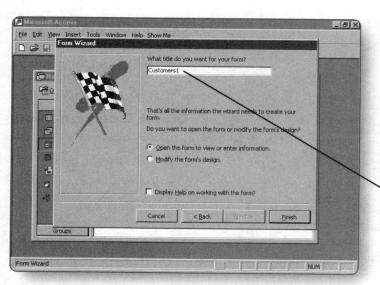

Finishing the Form

In the final step of the Form Wizard, you enter a form title and determine how to display your finished form.

1. Enter the **title** you want to display on your form in the text box.

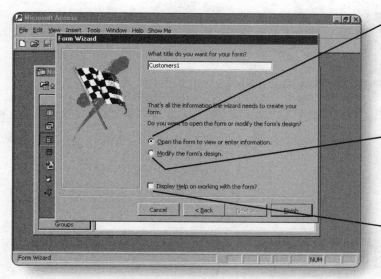

2a. Click on the **Open the Form to view or enter information option button**. The form will open in Form View.

OR

2b. Click on the **Modify the form's design option button**. The form will open in Design View.

3. Click on the **Display Help on working with the Form check box** if you want to automatically open a help window.

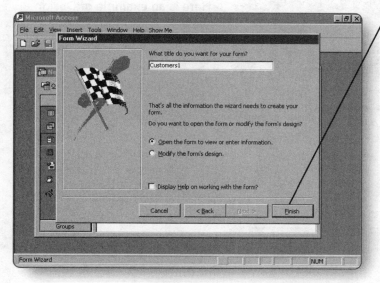

4. Click on **Finish**. Depending on the option you selected in step 2, Access will either display the form in Form View or Design View.

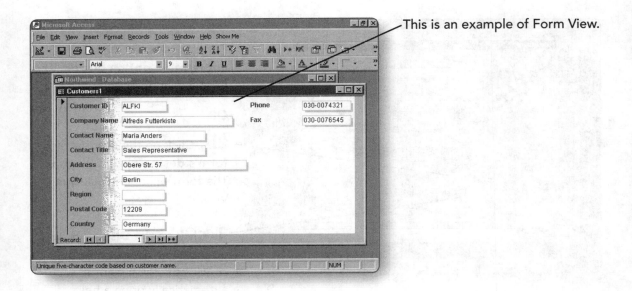

This is an example of Form View.

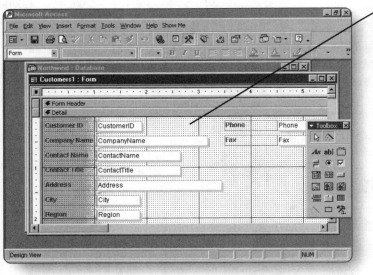

Here is an example of Design View.

14

Changing a Form's Appearance

After you create a form with the Form Wizard or AutoForm feature, you can change its default style or customize its formatting. In this chapter, you will learn how to:

- Open a form in Design View
- Change a form's format
- Modify fonts
- Bold, italicize, and underline
- Set alignment

Opening a Form in Design View

To modify the design of an existing form, open it in Design View. In this view you can apply a special format; modify fonts; bold, italicize, or underline text; set alignment; and more.

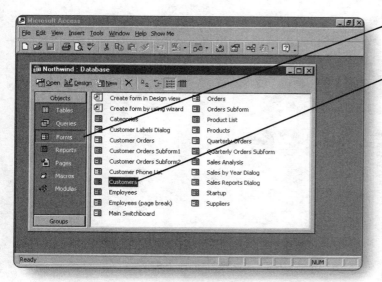

1. Click on the **Forms button** in the main database window.

2. Click on the **form you want to modify**. It will be highlighted.

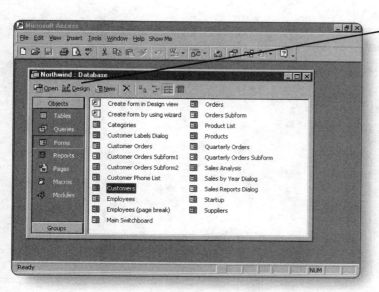

3. Click on the **Design button**. The form will open in Design View.

NOTE

Immediately open a form in Design View by choosing the Modify the form's design option button on the final Form Wizard step.

The first time you view a form in Design View, you'll notice that a form consists of controls placed in specific sections.

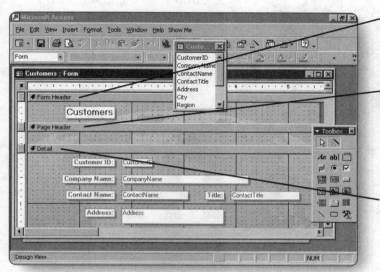

A form header displays information, such as labels, at the top of a form.

A page header displays information at the top each page of a form if, for instance, your form includes multiple pages.

Every form includes a detail section.

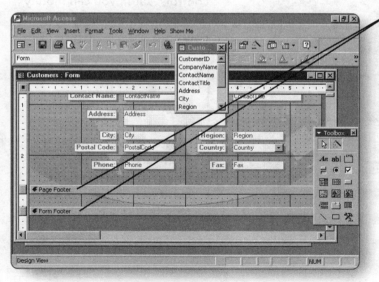

You can also include a page footer and form footer on a form. These work in the same way as a page or form header, but display in the lower portion, or footer, of the form.

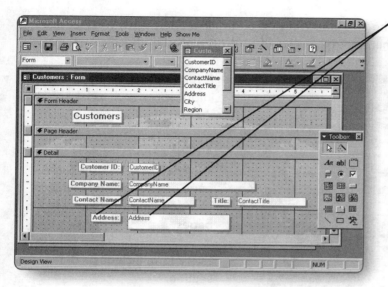

Labels and text boxes are examples of form controls. The Form Wizard and AutoForm features automatically create form sections and place controls in the appropriate location.

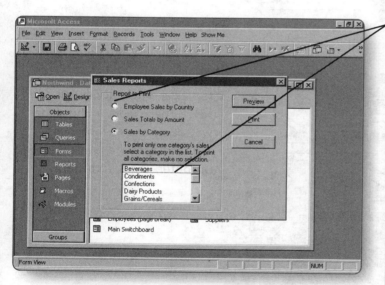

Option buttons and list boxes are also examples of form controls. Later, you can modify form controls manually or create new ones.

TIP

If you're new to Access, it's often easier to just create a new form rather than make extensive changes. Creating form controls or making major modifications to them is an advanced feature of Access.

Changing a Form's Format

The Form Wizard and AutoForm features help you choose a style or AutoFormat to apply to your form. AutoFormat uses predefined colors, borders, fonts, and font sizes designed to look good together and convey a specific image. You can always change the AutoFormat if you don't like the default or the style you originally chose.

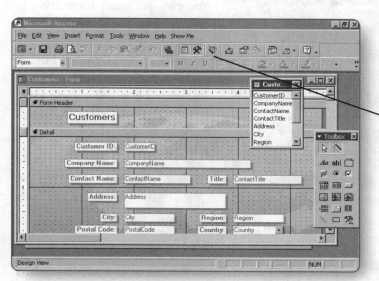

1. Click on the **AutoFormat button**. The AutoFormat dialog box will open with the current format highlighted.

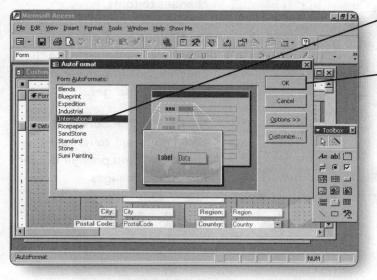

2. Click on a **new form format** in the Form AutoFormats list.

3. Click on **OK** to apply the new format.

Selecting Specific Formatting Options

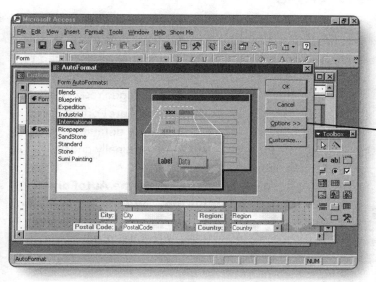

The AutoFormat default is to apply formatting to all the fonts, colors, and borders on a form. You can also apply formatting to only specific parts of the form.

1. Click on the **Options button** in the AutoFormat dialog box. The dialog box will extend to include the Attributes to Apply group box. By default, all attributes are selected.

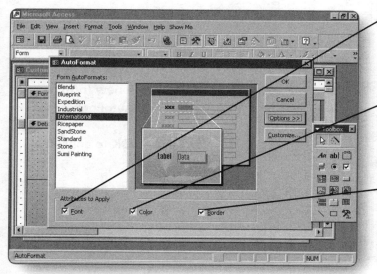

2. Click on the **Font check box** if you want to remove the check mark and prevent formatting changes to fonts.

3. Click on the **Color check box** if you want to remove the check mark and prevent color formatting changes.

4. Click on the **Border check box** if you want to remove the check mark and prevent border formatting changes.

Changing Fonts

You can change the fonts of individual controls on a form, such as labels or text boxes.

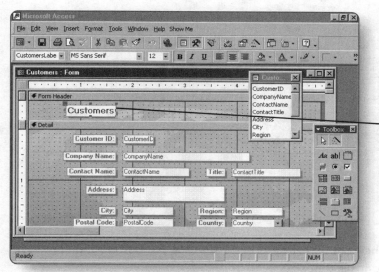

Changing Font Style

The Font drop-down list on the Formatting toolbar controls your form's fonts.

1. Click on the **control** whose font you want to change. Handles will surround this control to indicate that it is selected.

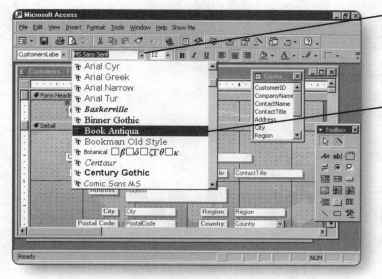

2. Click on the **down arrow** to the right of the Font list box on the Formatting toolbar. A menu will open.

3. Click on a **new font**.

CAUTION

It's fun to experiment with fonts, but remember that too many different fonts on the same form can become confusing for the user.

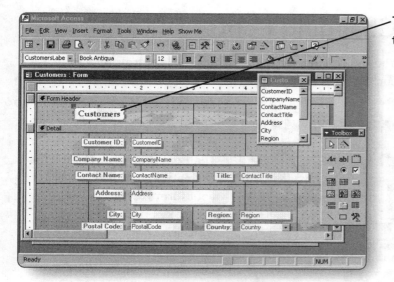

The control text will appear in the new font.

Changing Font Size

The Font Size drop-down list on the Formatting toolbar controls font size.

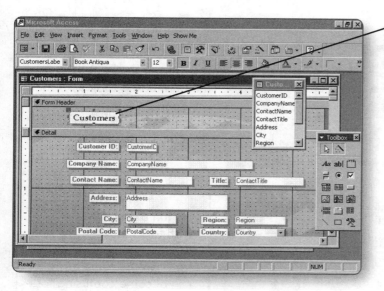

1. Click on the **control** whose font size you want to change. Handles will surround this control to indicate that it is selected.

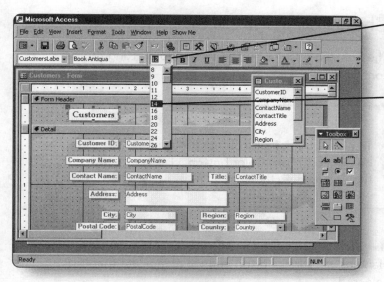

2. Click on the **down arrow** to the right of the font size list box. A menu will appear.

3. Click on a **new font size**.

TIP

Font sizes range from 8 to 72 points.

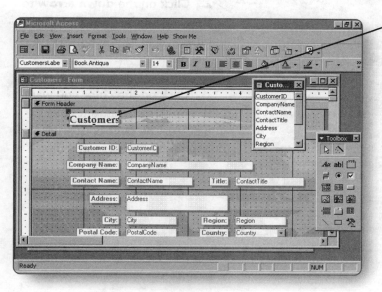

The control text will appear in the new font size.

Changing Font Color

The Font/Fore Color button on the Formatting toolbar controls font color.

> **TIP**
> To apply the default color that displays on the Font/Fore Color button, click on the button directly.

1. **Click** on the **control** whose font color you want to modify. Handles will surround this control to indicate that it is selected.

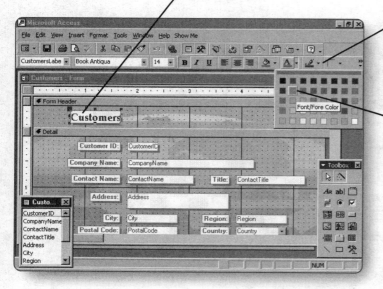

2. **Click** on the **down arrow** to the right of the Font/Fore Color button. The font color palette will open.

3. **Click** on the **color** you want to apply from the font color palette. The control text will appear in the new font color.

Bolding, Italicizing, and Underlining

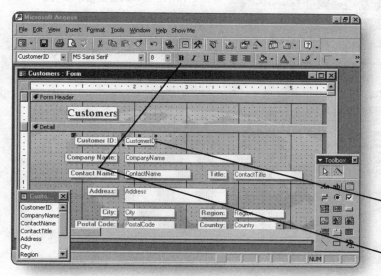

You can also modify the appearance of a form by bolding, italicizing, and underlining controls that contain text.

Bolding Text

The Bold button on the Formatting toolbar bolds text.

1. Click on the **control** you want to bold. It will be selected.

2. Click on the **Bold button**.

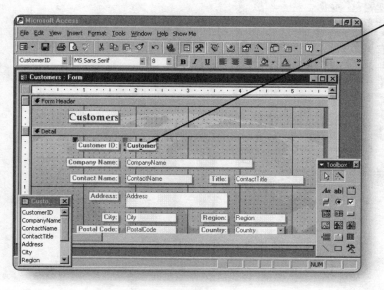

The control text will appear bolded.

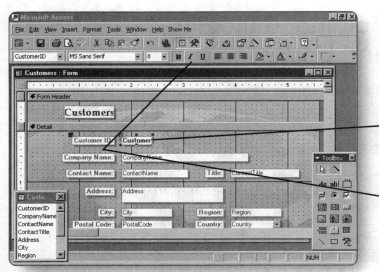

Italicizing Text

The Italic button on the Formatting toolbar italicizes text.

1. Click on the **control** you want to italicize. It will be selected.

2. Click on the **Italic button**.

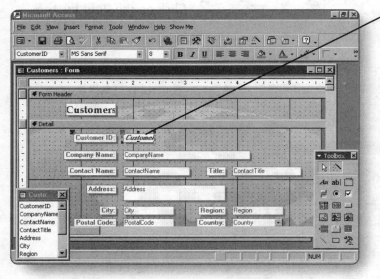

The control text will appear italicized.

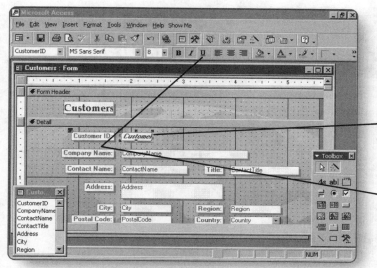

Underlining Text

The Underline button on the Formatting toolbar underlines text.

1. Click on the **control** you want to underline. It will be selected.

2. Click on the **Underline button**.

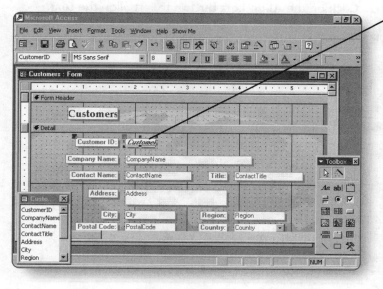

The control text will appear underlined.

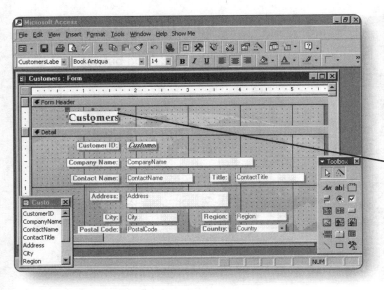

Setting Alignment

On Access forms, you can align controls to the left, center, or right.

1. Click on the **control** whose alignment you want to set.

2a. Click on the **Align Left button** to left align the text.

OR

2b. Click on the **Align Center button** to center the selected text.

OR

2c. Click on the **Align Right button** to right align the text. The control will be aligned.

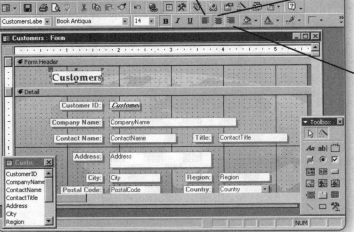

15

Adding Controls to Forms

In Design View you can further customize your form by adding fields and controls such as option groups, combo boxes, and list boxes. In this chapter, you will learn how to:

- Add form controls in Design View
- Add fields to forms
- Add option groups

Adding Form Controls in Design View

After you create a form with the Form Wizard or AutoForm feature, you'll probably make minor modifications to its appearance. You may also want to add additional fields to the form or add controls, such as list boxes, combo boxes, or option groups. To add additional controls to a form, you'll open it in Design View.

CAUTION

If you need to add more than one or two additional fields or controls, it's usually easier to create a new form. Making major form modifications takes a lot of time and can often lead to frustration.

---

1. Click on the **Forms button** in the main database window.

2. Click on the **form** that you want to modify. It will be highlighted.

3. Click on the **Design button**. The form will open in Design View.

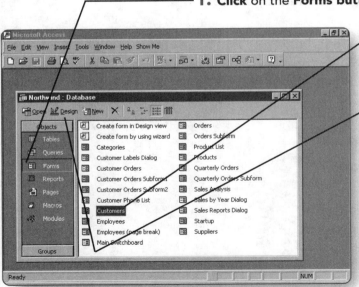

NOTE

Immediately open a form in Design View by choosing the Modify the form's design option button on the final Form Wizard step.

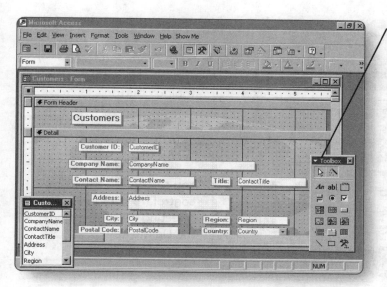

When you open a form in Design View, you'll see the Form Design Toolbox, which contains a series of buttons to help you create form controls.

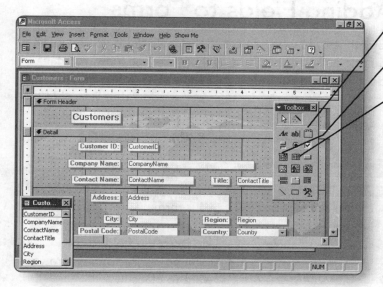

The Option Group button

The Combo Box button

The List Box button

These are examples of Toolbox buttons that create form controls. These buttons open wizards that guide you through control creation; others simply place a control directly on the form. Form controls serve several functions. Some, like labels or images, are informational or merely decorative. Others, like text box controls, enable users to either view or enter table field data. Other controls enable users to make choices, such as an option group.

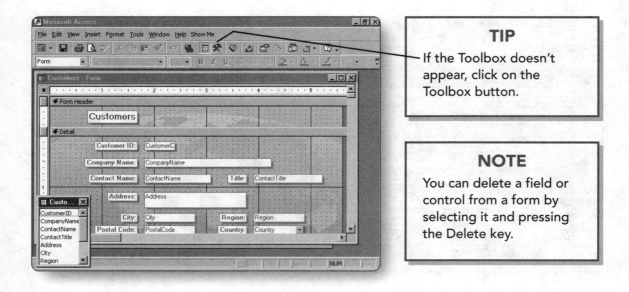

TIP

If the Toolbox doesn't appear, click on the Toolbox button.

NOTE

You can delete a field or control from a form by selecting it and pressing the Delete key.

Adding Fields to Forms

Sometimes you won't select all the table fields you need when you originally create a form. In Form Design View, you can add a new field control to your form through the field list, a small window that lists all of the table or query fields available for use with the form.

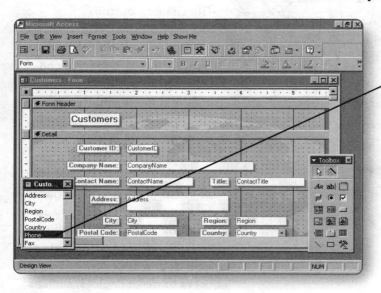

1. Click on the **field** in the field list that you want to include on your form.

2. Drag the **field** to the location on the form where you want to place it.

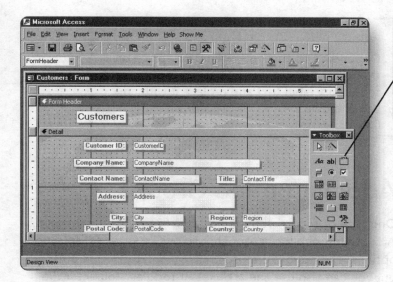

TIP

If the field list window doesn't display, click on the Field List button.

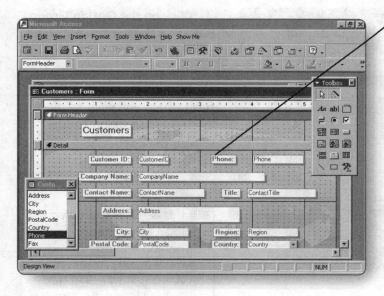

A control for that field will appear on the form.

NOTE

Most fields display as text box controls, but there are some exceptions. Yes/No fields display as check boxes, OLE fields display as bound object frames, and Lookup fields display as list boxes.

TIP

Depending on the kind of field you place on the form, you may need to select the temporary label text and replace it with an actual label.

Adding Option Groups

One type of control you can add to a form is an option group. An option group lets a user choose one of several displayed options. The options are usually preceded by option buttons, but you can also use check boxes or toggles. You enter the actual options as label names for the option group.

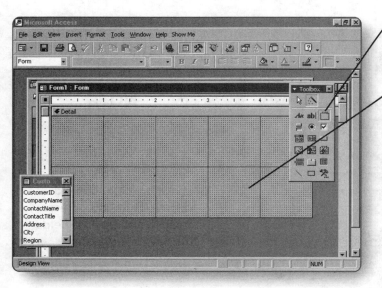

1. Click on the **Option Group button** in the Toolbox to activate it.

2. Click on the **area of the form** where you want to place the box. The Option Group Wizard will open.

TIP

If this is the first time you add an option group to a form and you use the default install, Access may prompt you to install this feature. Insert your Office 2000 program CD into your CD-ROM drive, and click on Yes to install.

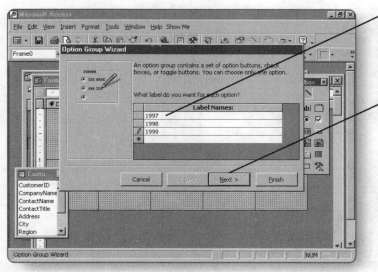

3. Type in the **label name** for each option button you want to display in the text box in the Label Names column.

4. Click on **Next** to continue.

Specifying a Default Choice

You can indicate a default option that will display for every record, but it isn't required.

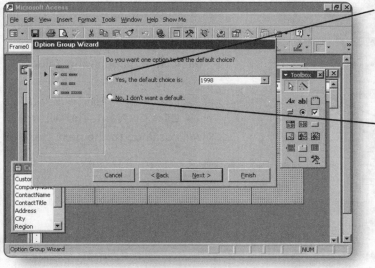

1a. Choose a **Field** in the drop-down list next to the Yes, the Default choice is option button to indicate the default.

OR

1b. Click on the **No, I don't want a default option button**.

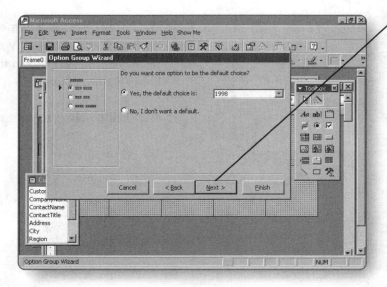

2. **Click** on **Next** to continue.

Setting Option Values

You assign a numeric value to each option in an option group. Access then saves this numeric value for later use or stores it in a table. The default numeric value series is 1, 2, 3, and so on.

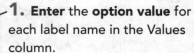

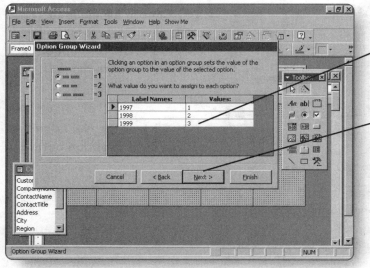

1. **Enter** the **option value** for each label name in the Values column.

2. **Click** on **Next**. The wizard will continue to the next step.

Saving or Storing the Option Group Value

You can either save the option group value for future use or store it in another form field.

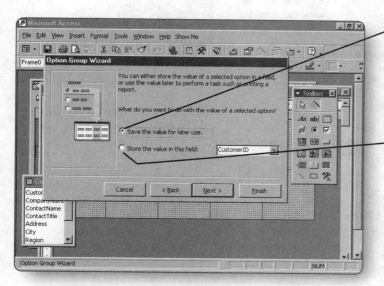

1a. **Click** on the **Save the value for later use option button** to save the value in memory for future use.

OR

1b. **Choose** a **field** in the drop-down list next to the Store the value in this field option button to indicate where to store the value.

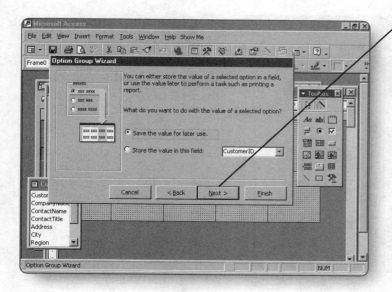

2. **Click** on **Next** to continue.

Specifying Controls and Styles

You can display your options as option buttons, check boxes, or toggle buttons. You can also choose one of five different box styles.

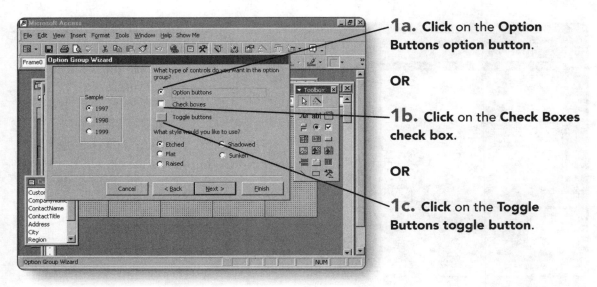

1a. Click on the **Option Buttons option button**.

OR

1b. Click on the **Check Boxes check box**.

OR

1c. Click on the **Toggle Buttons toggle button**.

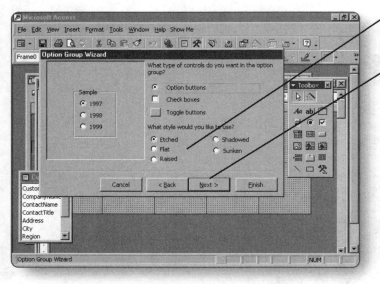

2. Click on the **option button** of the style you prefer.

3. Click on **Next** to continue to the final step.

Finishing the Option Group

In the final step of the Option Group Wizard, you'll create a label for the option group and specify help options.

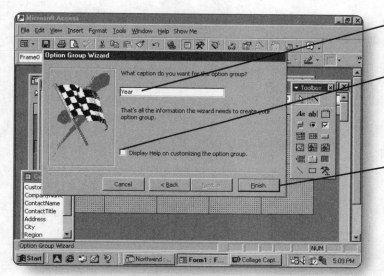

1. Enter a **name** for your option group in the text box.

2. Click on the **Display Help on customizing the option group check box** if you want to display a help window.

3. Click on **Finish**.

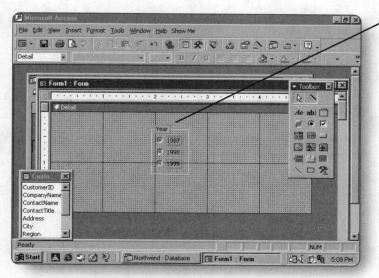

The option group will appear on the form.

16

Adding Combo and List Boxes to Forms

In Form Design View, you can use combo boxes and list boxes to enable users to select and enter data. In this chapter, you will learn how to:

- Understand combo boxes and list boxes
- Create a combo box or list box that will look up values
- Create a combo or list box in which you enter values
- Create a combo or list box that finds a record in the form

Understanding Combo and List Boxes

Access Form Design includes wizards that help you add list boxes and combo boxes to your forms.

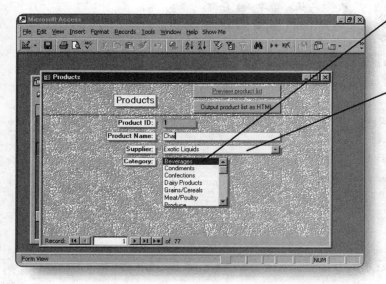

A list box control creates a list box from which the user can select one of the listed values.

A combo box control creates a list box of choices, but adds the flexibility of allowing the user to type in a specific value. You can create combo boxes or list boxes that work in different ways. The box can:

- Look up values in another table or query. For example, you might want to create a control that lists all the values of the CustomerName field in a Customer table.

- Display a list of values that you enter. In this type of control, you enter whatever values you want and you aren't limited to what already exists in a table or query.

- Find a record in your form that's based on the value you select in your combo or list box.

Creating Combo or List Boxes That Look Up Values

A wizard will guide you through the process of creating combo or list boxes that will look up values in a specified table or query.

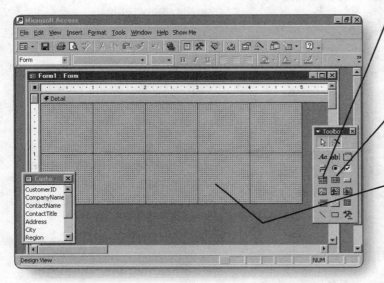

1a. Click on the **Combo Box button** in the Toolbox to activate it.

OR

1b. Click on the **List Box button** in the Toolbox to activate it.

2. Click on the **area of the form** where you want to place the box. The Combo Box Wizard or List Box Wizard will open, depending on your selection in step 1.

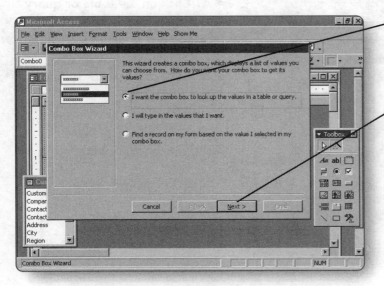

3. Click on the **I want the combo box (or list box) to look up the values in a table or query option button**.

4. Click on **Next** to continue.

Choosing a Table or Query

Next, you'll choose a table or query that contains the combo box or list box values.

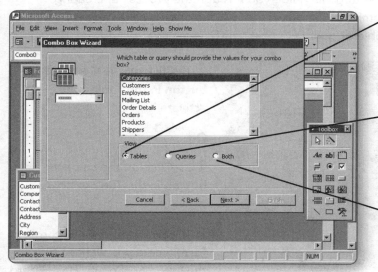

1a. **Click** on the **Tables option button** in the View group box to display only tables.

OR

1b. **Click** on the **Queries option button** in the View group box to display only queries.

OR

1c. **Click** on the **Both option button** in the View group box to display both tables and queries.

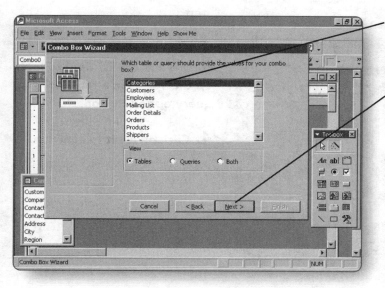

2. **Click** on the **table or query** that contains the values for the combo box or list box.

3. **Click** on **Next** to continue.

Selecting Fields

Next, you'll select the fields to include as combo box or list box columns.

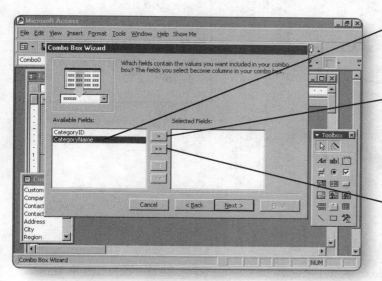

1. **Choose** the **first field** that you want to include from the Available Fields list.

2. **Click** on the **right arrow button**. The field will move to the Selected Fields list.

TIP

Click on the double right arrow button to include all available fields in your combo box or list box.

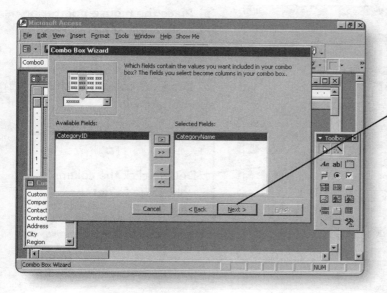

3. **Repeat steps 1** and **2** until you select all the fields that you want to include in your combo box or list box.

4. **Click** on **Next**. The wizard will continue to the next step.

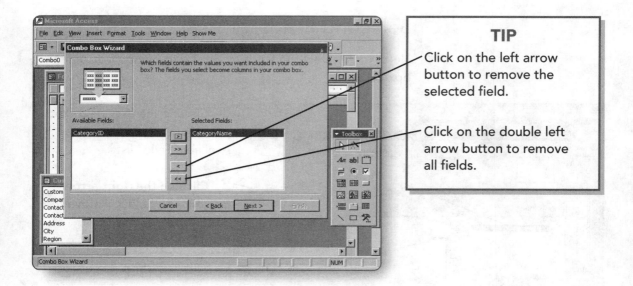

TIP

Click on the left arrow button to remove the selected field.

Click on the double left arrow button to remove all fields.

Specifying Column Width

Next, you'll specify how wide to make the columns in your combo box or list box.

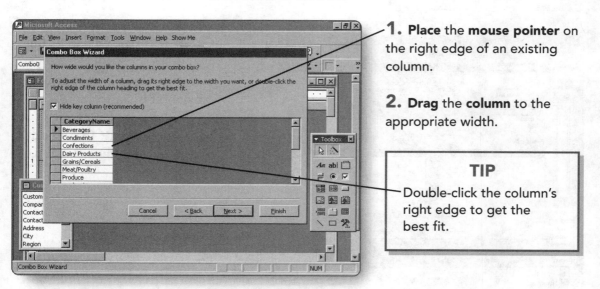

1. Place the **mouse pointer** on the right edge of an existing column.

2. Drag the **column** to the appropriate width.

TIP

Double-click the column's right edge to get the best fit.

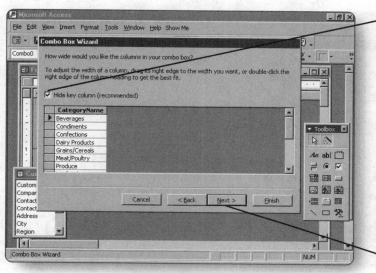

3. Click on the **Hide key column (recommended) check box** to hide the primary key column.

NOTE

You'll usually want to hide the primary key column because it doesn't contain actual data.

4. Click on **Next** to continue.

Determining What to Do with the Value

You can either save the combo box or list box value for future use or store it in another field.

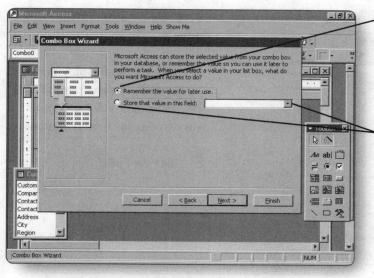

1a. Click on the **Remember the value for later use option button** to save the value in memory for future use.

OR

1b. Click on the **Store that value in this field option button,** and then click on the down arrow to the right of the text box. A menu will appear.

1c. Click on a **field** in which to store the value.

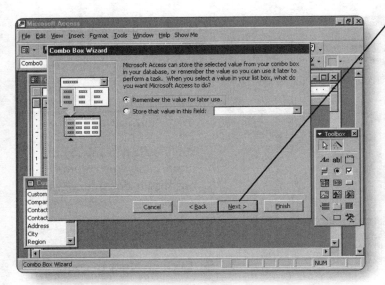

2. Click on **Next** to continue.

Finishing the Combo Box or List Box

In the final wizard step, you'll create a label for the combo box or list box.

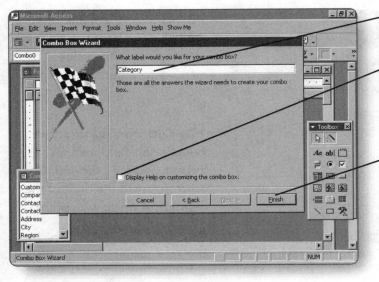

1. Enter a **name** for your box in the text box.

2. Click on the **Display Help on customizing the combo box (or list box) check box** if you want to display a help window.

3. Click on **Finish**.

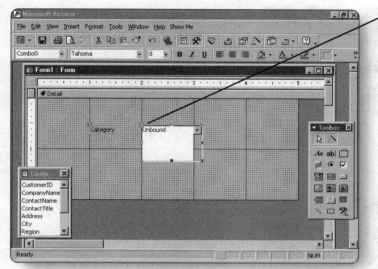

The box will appear on the form.

Creating a Combo Box or List Box in Which You Enter Values

You can also create a combo box or list box in which you can enter the box values directly rather than taking them from an existing report or query. For example, you may want to have users select from a list that displays the past three years, your company's branch locations, or the products you make.

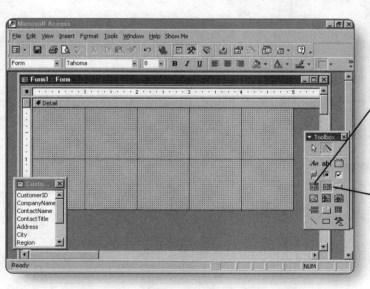

1a. Click on the **Combo Box button** in the Toolbox to activate it.

OR

1b. Click on the **List Box button** in the Toolbox to activate it.

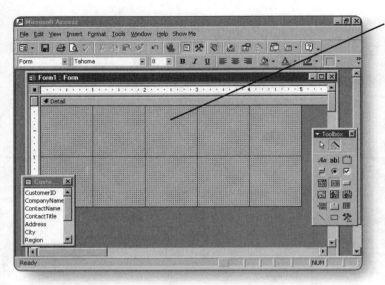

2. Click on the **area of the form** where you want to place the box. The wizard will open.

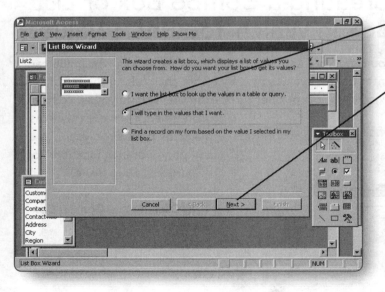

3. Click on the **I will type in the values that I want option button**.

4. Click on **Next** to continue.

Entering the Box Values

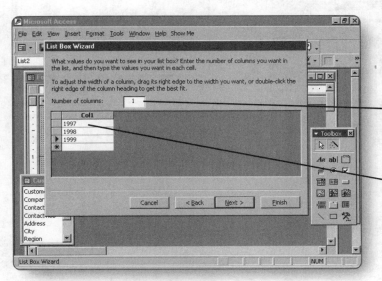

Next, you'll enter the values that you want to appear in the combo box or list box and adjust the column width.

1. Enter the **number of columns** you need in the Number of Columns text box.

2. Type in the **values** that you want to include in each column.

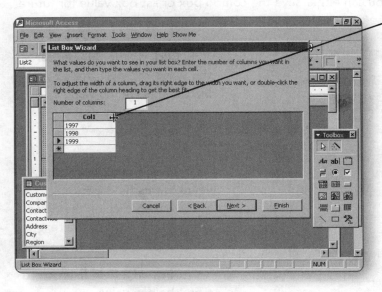

3. Place the **mouse pointer** on the right edge of the column that you want to adjust.

4. Drag the **column** to the appropriate width.

5. Repeat steps 3 and **4** until you adjust all necessary columns.

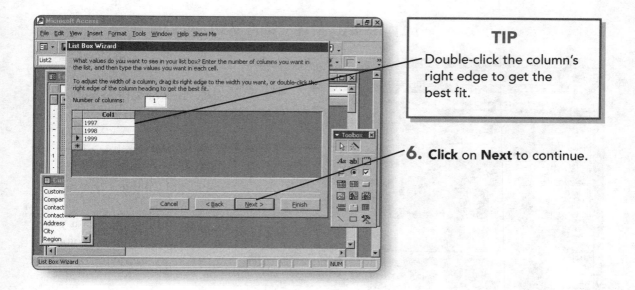

TIP

Double-click the column's right edge to get the best fit.

6. Click on **Next** to continue.

Saving or Storing the Box Value

You can either save the combo box or list box value for future use or store it in another field.

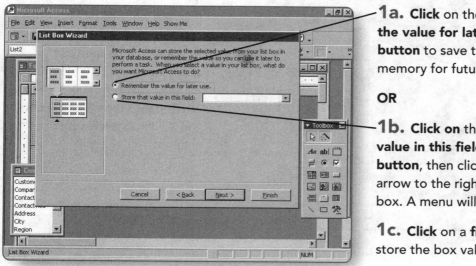

1a. Click on the **Remember the value for later use option button** to save the value in memory for future use.

OR

1b. Click on the **Store that value in this field option button**, then click on the down arrow to the right of the text box. A menu will appear.

1c. Click on a **field** in which to store the box value.

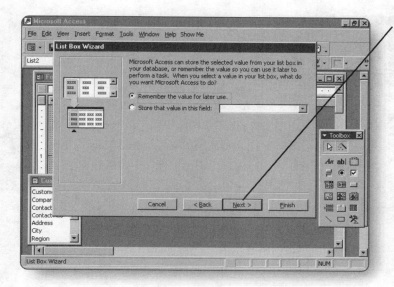

2. Click on **Next** to continue.

Finishing the Combo Box or List Box

In the final wizard step, you'll create a label and specify whether or not to open the help window.

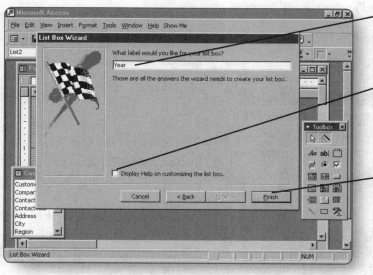

1. Enter a **name** for your combo box or list box in the text box.

2. Click on the **Display Help on customizing the combo box (or list box) check box** if you want to display a help window.

3. Click on **Finish**.

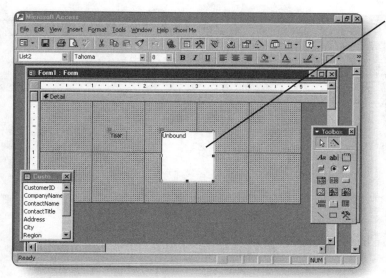

The box will appear in the form.

Creating a Combo Box or List Box That Finds a Record in the Form

Finally, you can create a combo box or list box that will locate a record in the current form.

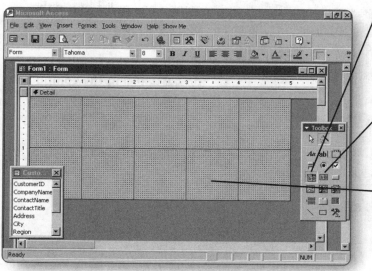

1a. Click on the **Combo Box button** in the Toolbox to activate it.

OR

1b. Click on the **List Box button** in the Toolbox to activate it.

2. Click on the **area of the form** where you want to place the combo box or list box. The wizard will open.

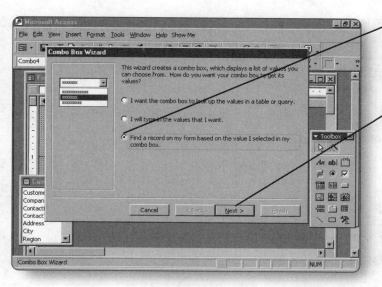

3. Click on the **Find a record on my form based on the value I selected in my combo box option button**.

4. Click on **Next** to continue.

Selecting Fields

Next, you'll select the fields to include.

1. Click on the **first field** that you want to include from the Available Fields list.

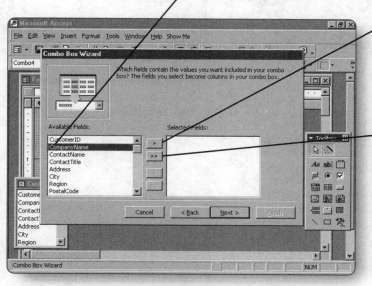

2. Click on the **right arrow button**. The field will move to the Selected Fields list.

TIP

Click on the double right arrow button to include all available fields in your box.

3. Repeat steps 1 and **2** until you select all the fields that you want to include in your combo box.

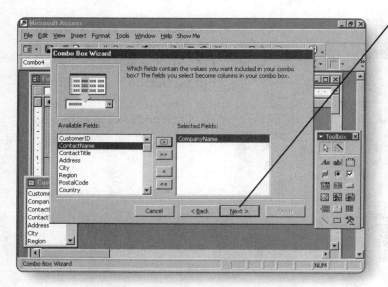

4. Click on **Next**. The wizard will continue to the next step.

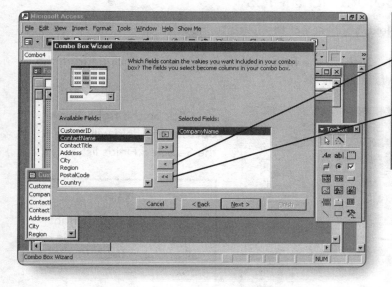

TIP

Click on the left arrow button to remove the selected field.

Click on the double left arrow button to remove all fields.

Specifying Column Width

Next, you will specify how wide to make the columns.

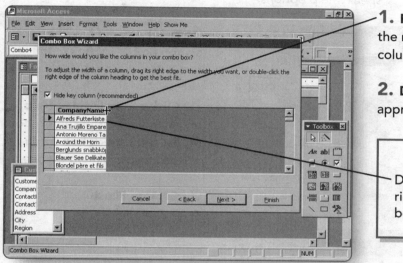

1. **Place** the **mouse pointer** on the right edge of an existing column.

2. **Drag** the **column** to the appropriate width.

TIP

Double-click the column's right edge to get the best fit.

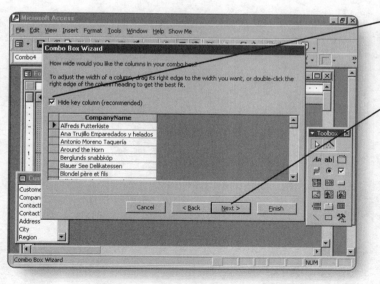

3. **Click** on the **Hide key column (recommended) check box** to hide the primary key column.

4. **Click** on **Next** to continue.

Finishing the Combo Box or List Box

In the final wizard step, you'll create a label for the box and specify help options.

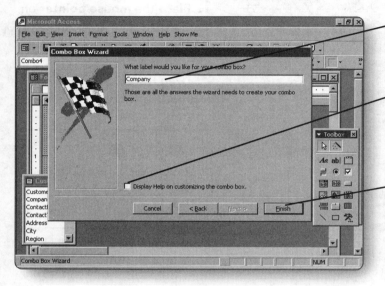

1. **Enter** a **name** for your combo box or list box in the text box.

2. **Click** on the **Display Help on customizing the combo box (or list box) check box** if you want to display a help window.

3. **Click** on **Finish**.

17

Entering Data in a Form

Forms offer an alternative way to enter data in Access tables. Using a form, you can enter data from a more visual perspective. You can also enter data in more than one table. In this chapter, you'll learn how to:

- Open a form in Form View
- Use edit mode to enter form data
- Use data entry mode to enter form data
- Save form data entries

Opening a Form in Form View

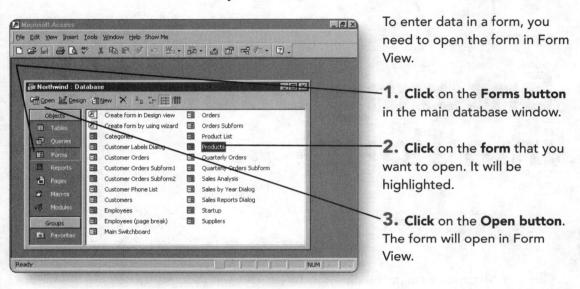

To enter data in a form, you need to open the form in Form View.

1. **Click** on the **Forms button** in the main database window.

2. **Click** on the **form** that you want to open. It will be highlighted.

3. **Click** on the **Open button**. The form will open in Form View.

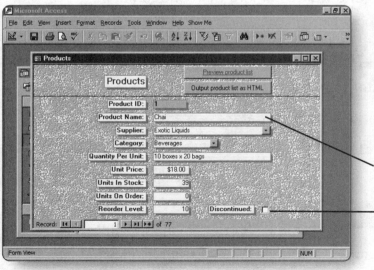

Form View offers an alternative, visual way to enter data into a table or tables. You enter data in forms through a number of form controls. The most common form controls you'll use to enter data include the following:

- **Text box**. Type an entry in the box.

- **Check box**. Click on the check box to select the field.

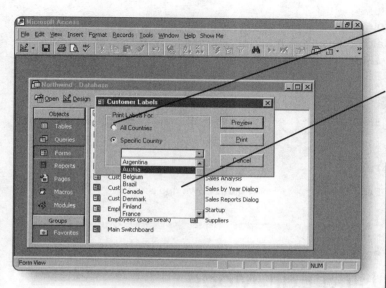

- **Option button**. Click on one of the available option buttons in an option group box.

- **Combo box**. Choose an entry from the drop-down list or type your own entry.

NOTE

You can also open a form in Form View directly from the Form Wizard by choosing the Enter data directly into the form option button on the final wizard step.

Navigating in Form View

The current form record number is displayed in the record number box at the bottom of the screen. Several navigation buttons surround this box. Using these buttons, you can move to the first, preceding, next, or last form record.

You can also use the mouse to navigate the form or select the field you want. In addition, Access provides several other form navigation commands:

Enter or Tab	Navigates to the next field.
Shift+Tab	Navigates to the preceding field.
Page Up	Navigates up one screen.
Page Down	Navigates down one screen.

Using Edit Mode to Enter Data in a Form

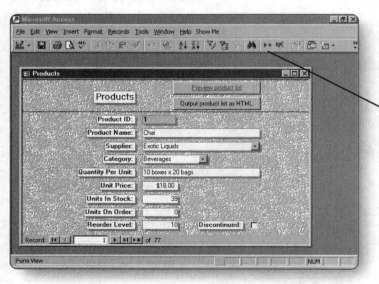

One way to enter data in a form is to use Edit mode, which creates a blank form after the last complete form record.

1. Click on the **New Record button**. A blank form record will appear.

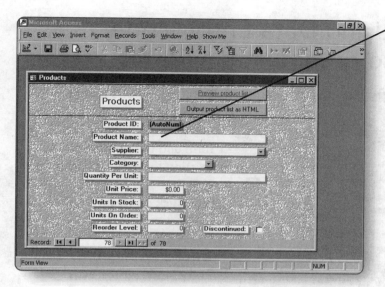

2. Enter data in the new form.

3. Repeat steps 1 and **2** until you finish adding data.

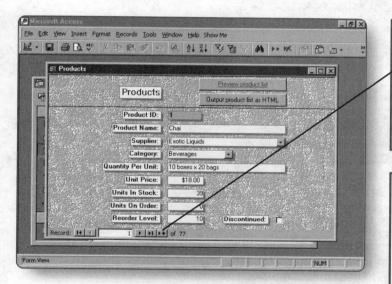

TIP

You can also click on the New Record button to the right of the navigation buttons to add a new record.

NOTE

Access automatically enters the next consecutive number in an AutoNumber field.

Using Data Entry Mode to Enter Data in Forms

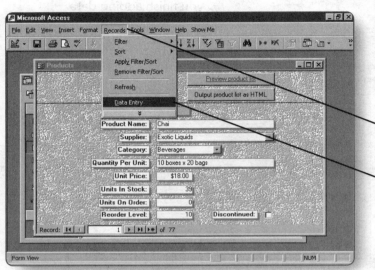

Data Entry mode is another way to enter data in a form. Data Entry mode displays a blank form and temporarily hides all existing form records from view.

1. Click on **Records**. The Records menu will appear.

2. Click on **Data Entry**. Data Entry mode will be activated.

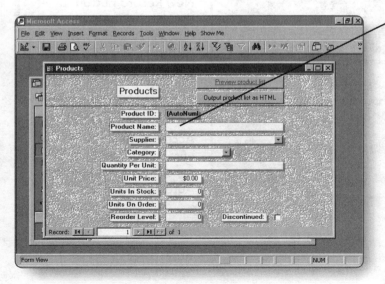

3. Enter data in the new blank form.

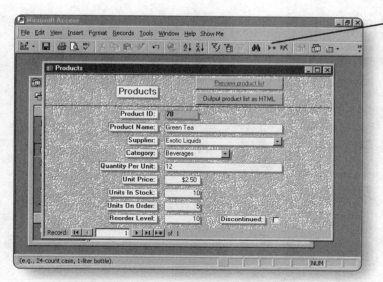

4. Click on the **New Record button** to open another blank form.

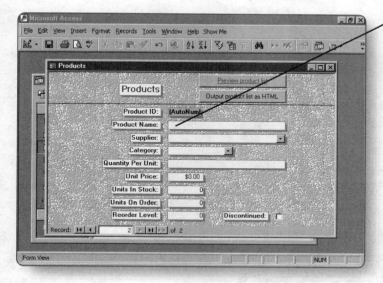

5. Enter data in this form.

6. Repeat steps 4 and **5** until you finish entering data.

Exiting Data Entry Mode

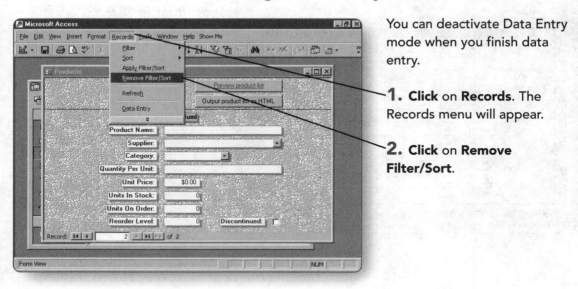

You can deactivate Data Entry mode when you finish data entry.

1. Click on **Records**. The Records menu will appear.

2. Click on **Remove Filter/Sort**.

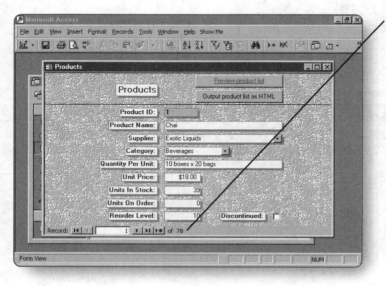

The hidden form records will appear again.

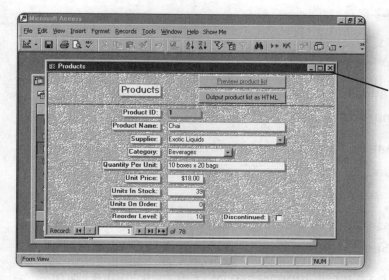

Saving Form Data Entries

To exit a form and save your entries, click on the Close button.

Part V Review Questions

1. How do you automatically create a form in a vertical format? *See "Creating a Columnar AutoForm" in Chapter 12*

2. What automated feature lets you create a form that displays your table data in rows and columns? *See "Creating a Tabular AutoFormat" in Chapter 12*

3. How can you get assistance in creating a form in which you choose fields and format? *See "Starting the Form Wizard" in Chapter 13*

4. Where do you set the overall appearance of your form in the Form Wizard? *See "Choosing a Form Style" in Chapter 13*

5. In which view do you open a form when you want to modify its appearance? *See "Opening a Form in Design View" in Chapter 14*

6. How to you change a form's AutoFormat? *See "Selecting Specific Formatting Options" in Chapter 14*

7. Where can you add form controls? *See "Adding Form Controls in Design View" in Chapter 15*

8. How can you add a drop-down list based on your own values to your form? *See "Creating a Combo Box or List Box in Which You Enter Values" in Chapter 16*

9. How do you enter data in a form? *See "Opening a Form in Form View" in Chapter 17*

10. Which mode temporarily hides all existing records while you enter data in a form? *See "Using Data Entry Mode to Enter Data in Forms" in Chapter 17*

PART VI

Querying for Information

18

Using the Simple Query Wizard

The Simple Query Wizard guides you through the creation of a basic select query that extracts specific fields from tables or other queries. In this chapter, you'll learn how to:

- Start the Simple Query Wizard
- Select fields
- Choose a detail or summary query
- Finish the query

Starting the Simple Query Wizard

The Simple Query Wizard helps you to create a simple select query from fields that you specify. In Access 2000, a select query selects data you choose from single or multiple tables or queries. For example, you could create a query that lists only certain fields in a table that contains a large number of fields.

NOTE

A query is a way to extract information from your database. You can create queries to select, analyze, and summarize specific data.

---

1. Click on the **Queries button** in the main database window.

2. Double-click on **Create query by using wizard** within the database window. The Simple Query Wizard will open.

Selecting Fields

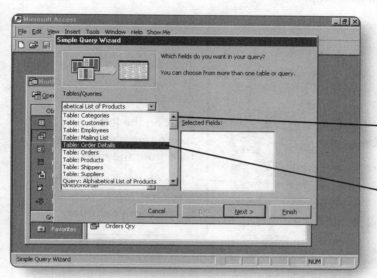

In the next step, you choose the specific fields to include in your query and indicate the table or other query in which they are located.

1. **Click** on the **down arrow** to the right of the Tables/Queries box. A menu will appear.

2. **Click on the table or query** from which you want to select your query field. A list of the fields for that table/query will appear.

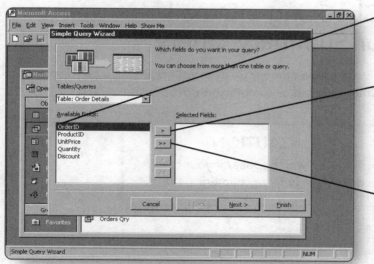

3. **Choose** the **first field that** you want to include in your query from the Available Fields list.

4. **Click** on the **right arrow button**. The field will move to the Selected Fields list.

TIP

You can quickly include all available fields by clicking on the double right arrow button.

5. **Repeat steps 1** through **3** until you have selected all fields to include in the query.

6. Click on **Next**. The Simple Query Wizard will continue to the next step.

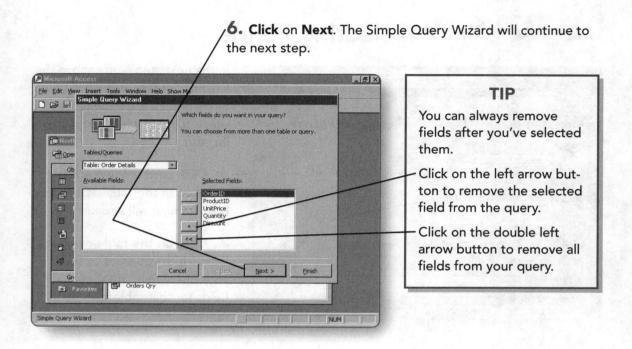

TIP

You can always remove fields after you've selected them.

Click on the left arrow button to remove the selected field from the query.

Click on the double left arrow button to remove all fields from your query.

Choosing a Detail or Summary Query

If you include number fields in your query, you can display either detailed or summary information.

CAUTION

This step won't appear if your query doesn't include any numeric fields.

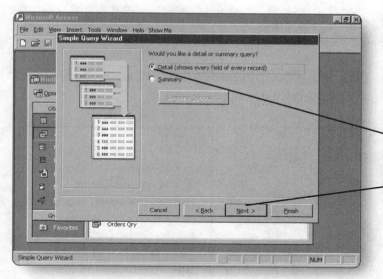

Creating a Detail Query

A detail query includes all fields in all records.

1. Click on the **Detail option button**.

2. Click on **Next** to continue.

Creating a Summary Query

A summary query lets you summarize information in your select query. Through the Summary Options dialog box, you can specify up to four different summary options for each numeric field in your query. These options include the ability to summarize a field as well as to display its average, minimum, or maximum.

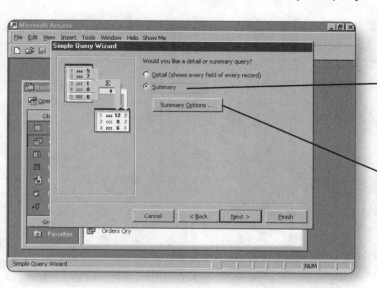

1. Click on the **Summary option button**. The Summary Options button will become active.

2. Click on the **Summary Options ... button**. The Summary Options dialog box will open.

3. Click on the **check box** for each field and summary option combination you want to include in your query.

4. Click on the **Count records in Order Details check box** to display the record count in the query.

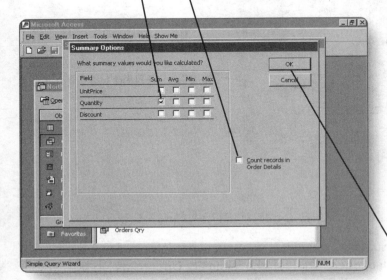

NOTE

In this example, the check box is named Count records in Order Details since the query is based on the Order Details table. The dialog box will substitute the name of whatever table you actually use to create your query.

5. Click on **OK** to return to the Simple Query Wizard.

6. Click on **Next** to continue to the next step.

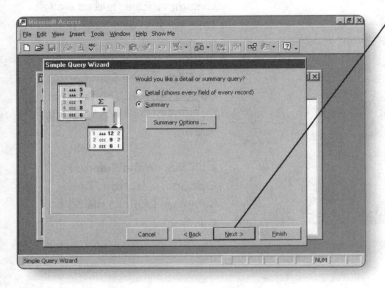

Finishing the Query

In the Simple Query Wizard's last step, you enter a query title and determine how to open the query.

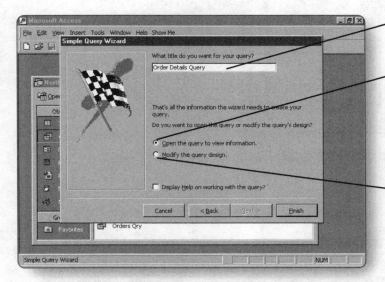

1. **Enter** a **name** for the query in the text box.

2a. **Click** on the **Open the query to view information option button** to open the query in Datasheet View.

OR

2b. **Click** on the **Modify the query design option button** to open the query in Design View.

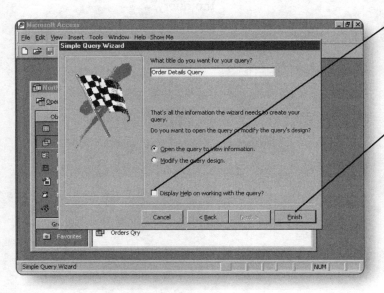

3. **Click** on the **Display Help on working with the query check box** to display the help window when you open the query.

4. **Click** on **Finish**. The query will open based on your selection in step 2.

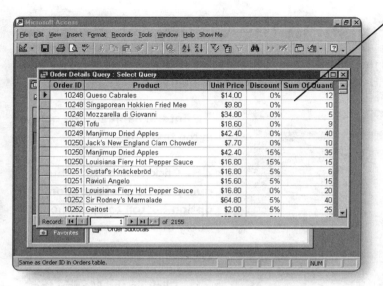

If you choose to open the query in this final wizard step, the query will display the fields you selected in Datasheet View.

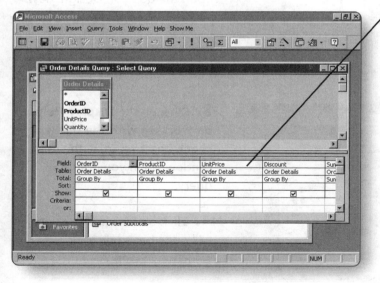

If you choose to modify the query's design in this step, it will open in Design View, in which you can modify and customize the query.

19

Using the Crosstab Query Wizard

The Crosstab Query Wizard helps you build a query that analyzes the data in a spreadsheet format and allows you to look at your table data in different ways. In this chapter, you'll learn how to:

- Start the Crosstab Query Wizard
- Select a table
- Select fields
- Select a column heading
- Select a summary method
- Finish the query

Starting the Crosstab Query Wizard

Using the Crosstab Query Wizard, you can summarize information in a spreadsheet format. Crosstab queries let you look at your table data in different ways.

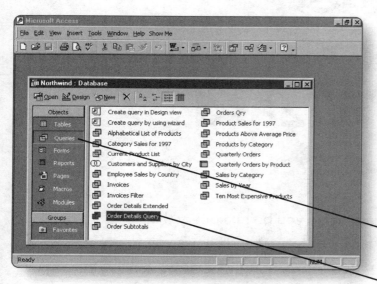

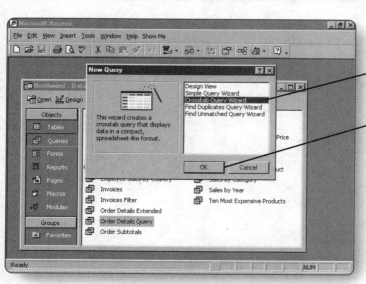

NOTE

If you're new to the concept of crosstab queries, it's a good idea to write your query format on paper before using the wizard. Remember, a crosstab query looks like a spreadsheet.

1. Click on the **Queries button** in the main database window.

2. Click on the **New button**. The New Query dialog box will open.

3. Click on the **Crosstab Query Wizard** option.

4. Click on **OK**. The Crosstab Query Wizard will open.

Selecting a Table or Query

You can base your crosstab query on either a table or another query.

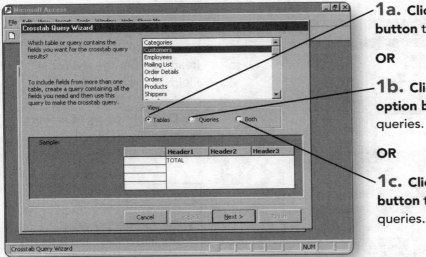

1a. Click on the **Tables option button** to view only tables.

OR

1b. Click on the **Queries option button** to view only queries.

OR

1c. Click on the **Both option button** to view both tables and queries.

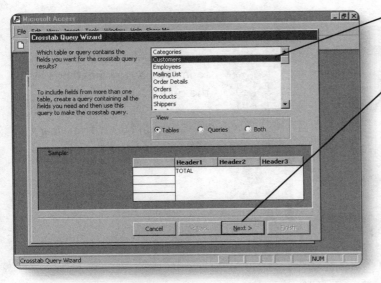

2. Click on the **table or query** on which you want to base your crosstab query.

3. Click on **Next**.

Selecting Row Heading Fields

In a crosstab query, you can select up to three fields to be the row headings—just as in a spreadsheet. The order in which you select these fields is the order in which they are sorted.

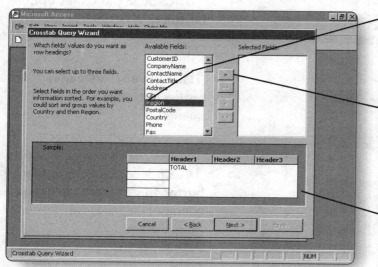

1. Choose the **first field** that you want to include as a row heading from the Available Fields scroll box.

2. Click on the **right arrow button**. The field will move to the Selected Fields scroll box.

NOTE
The sample preview box illustrates how your crosstab query will actually look.

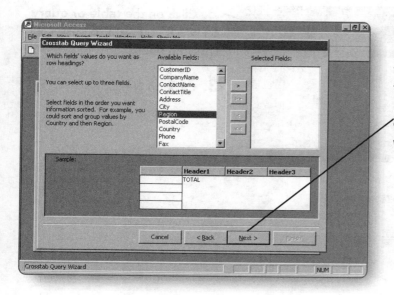

3. Repeat steps 1 and **2** until you select all the fields you want to include as row headings in the query.

4. Click on **Next**. The wizard will continue to the next step.

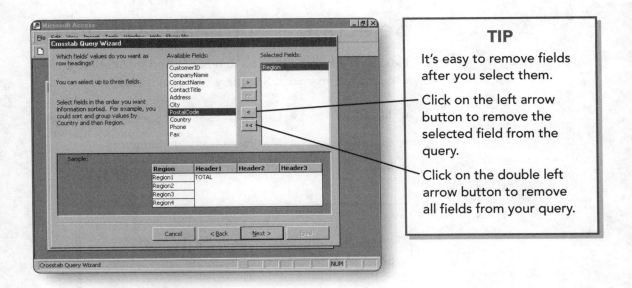

TIP

It's easy to remove fields after you select them.

Click on the left arrow button to remove the selected field from the query.

Click on the double left arrow button to remove all fields from your query.

Selecting a Column Heading

Next, you'll select one field to be the column heading in the crosstab query.

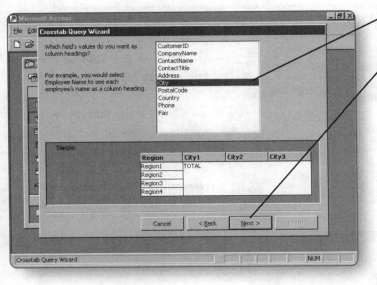

1. Choose the **field** to be the column heading.

2. Click on **Next** to continue to the next step.

Selecting a Summary Method

Next, you'll select a field to summarize and the method by which to summarize it. Summary options include:

- Average
- Count
- First
- Last
- Maximum
- Minimum
- Standard Deviation
- Summary
- Variance

NOTE
Only numeric fields will display in the Fields list because only numeric fields can be summarized.

TIP
Depending on the types of fields you use in your query, not all summary options are available.

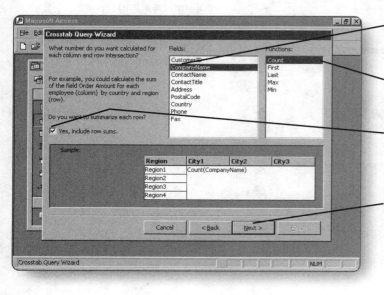

1. Click on the **field to summarize** from the Fields list.

2. Click on the **summary method** from the Functions list.

3. Click on the **Yes, include row sums check box** if you want to summarize each row.

4. Click on **Next** to continue.

Finishing the Query

You'll enter a query title and determine how to open the query in this last step. You can either view the query results or open the query in Design View to make further modifications.

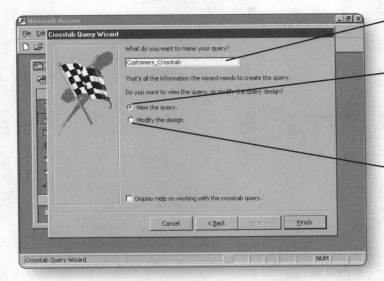

1. Enter a **name** for the query in the text box.

2a. Click on the **View the query option button** to open the query in Datasheet View.

OR

2b. Click on the **Modify the design option button** to open the query in Design View.

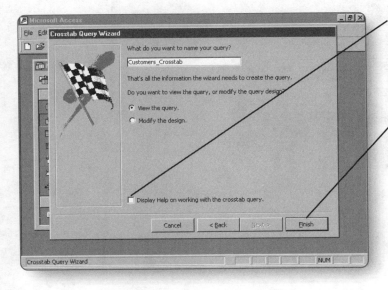

3. Click on the **Display Help on working with the crosstab query check box** if you want to have help when you open the query.

4. Click on **Finish**. The crosstab query will open based on your choice in step 2.

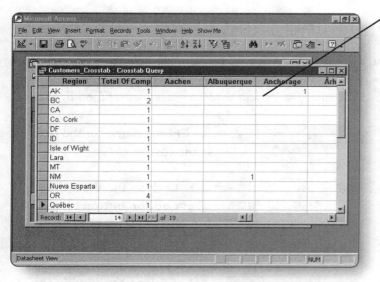

If you choose to view the query in this final wizard step, you'll see the end results of the crosstab query which crosstabulates your data into a spreadsheet format.

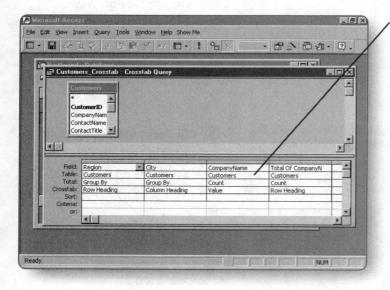

If you choose to, you can further modify and customize the query's design in this step.

20

Creating Queries in Design View

If you want more flexibility than a query wizard provides, you can create a query from scratch in Design View. In this chapter, you will learn how to:

- Start a query in Design View
- Select a table
- Add fields
- Specify criteria
- Specify calculations
- View query results
- Save a query

Starting a Query in Design View

To create a query from scratch, you need to start it in Design View.

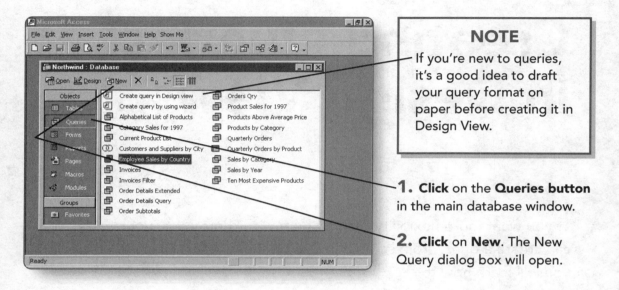

NOTE

If you're new to queries, it's a good idea to draft your query format on paper before creating it in Design View.

1. Click on the **Queries button** in the main database window.

2. Click on **New**. The New Query dialog box will open.

TIP

You can also open the New Query dialog box by double-clicking on the Create query in Design View option in the database window.

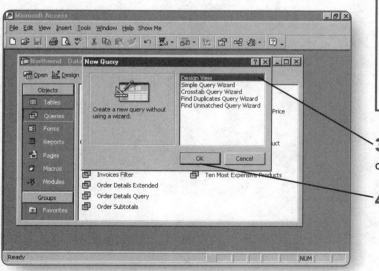

3. Click on the **Design View** option.

4. Click on **OK**.

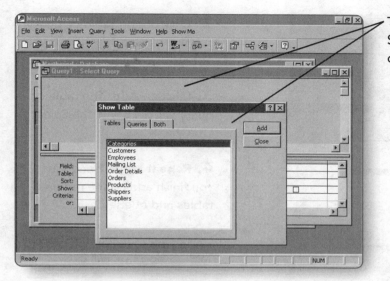

The Select Query window and Show Table dialog box will open.

Selecting a Table or Query

You can include fields from other tables or queries in your new query by selecting them in the Show Table dialog box.

1a. Click on the **Tables tab** to view only tables.

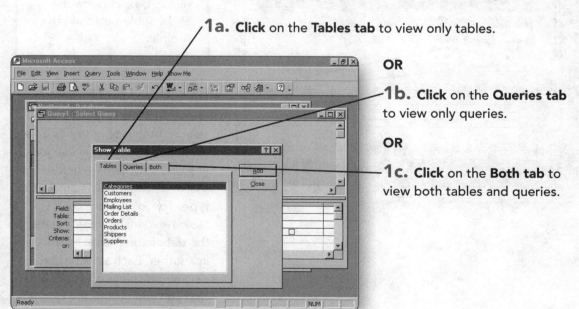

OR

1b. Click on the **Queries tab** to view only queries.

OR

1c. Click on the **Both tab** to view both tables and queries.

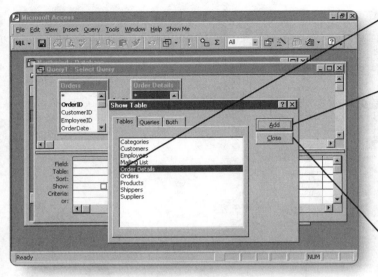

2. Click on the **table or query** you want to include in your new query.

3. Click on **Add**. The table or query will display in the Select Query window.

4. Repeat steps 2 and **3** until you finish adding the required tables and queries.

5. Click on **Close**. The Show Table dialog box will close.

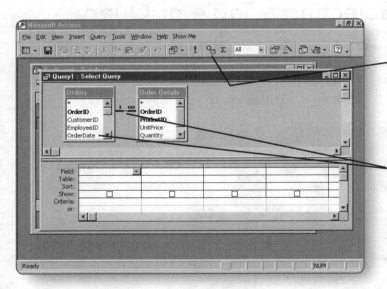

TIP

To reopen the Show Table dialog box, click on the Show Table button in the toolbar.

The top portion of the Select Query window displays each selected table or query as a field list joined by a line. These *join lines* link *key fields*—fields that share the same field name and type. The join lines indicate table relationships that relate the data in one table to the data in another. Each selected table or query displays a list of fields that you can add to the query.

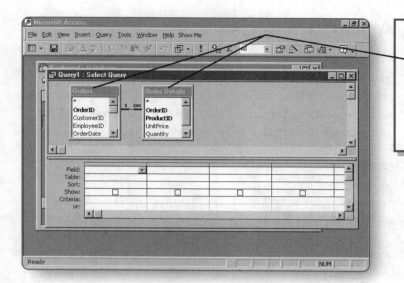

TIP

To link key fields manually, click on a field in one list box and drag it to the other linking field in another field list.

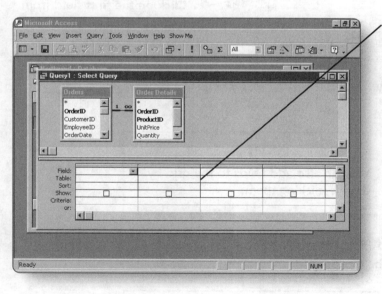

The bottom portion of the Select Query window displays the *design grid*. You'll add fields to the query by dragging them from the field lists to the design grid. The design grid is similar to a spreadsheet, with columns representing each field in the query.

Adding Fields

To add fields to your query, you'll drag them to the design grid. Once you place a field in the design grid, the Field row will display the field name, the Table row will display the original table, and the Show row will display a check mark. All fields with a check mark in the Show row will display in your query.

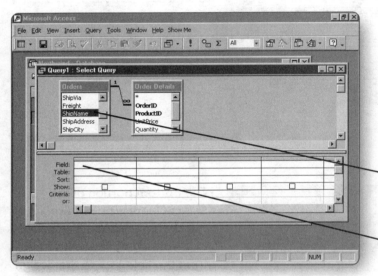

TIP

Remove the check mark from the Show check box to temporarily hide the field from the query results.

1. Click on the **first field** from the field list that you want to include in your query.

2. Drag the **selected field** to a Field row in the design grid.

TIP

You can also add fields to the grid by double-clicking them.

3. Repeat steps 1 and **2** until you add all desired fields to the design grid.

TIP

To add all fields in a field list to the query, double-click on the field list and drag it to the design grid.

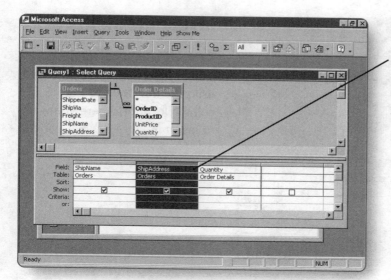

Deleting Fields

If you want to delete a field from the design grid, click on the field selector for that field, then press the Delete key on your keyboard.

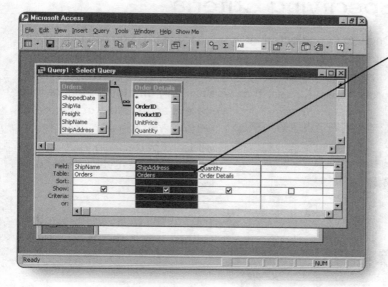

Moving Fields

To move a field on the design grid, click on the field selector for that field. The field column will be highlighted. Drag it to the new location.

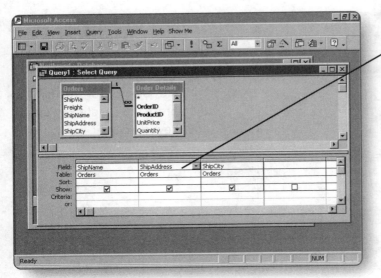

Inserting Fields

To insert a field between two existing fields in the design grid, drag the new field to the column location where you want to insert it.

Specifying Criteria

Once you've selected all your query fields, you can narrow your query to include only data that matches specific criteria. You may want to display only records with certain field values, for example. A query that displays only employees in a certain state is an example of the use of criteria. You can also use wildcard patterns in your criteria or indicate what values *not* to include.

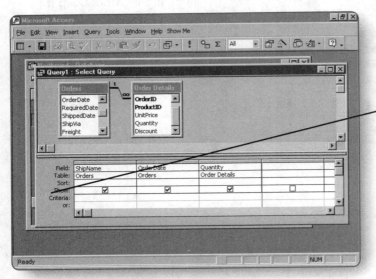

You specify query criteria in the Criteria row in the design grid.

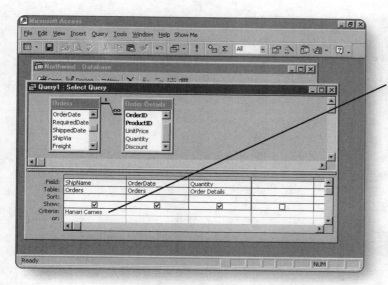

Specifying Exact Matches

To specify an exact match, you'll enter an exact value in the Criteria row of the field column in which you want to search.

Specifying Wildcard Patterns

Wildcards offer a way of setting criteria based on patterns or partial words rather than exact matches.

The most common wildcard operators include:

? Replaces a single character

* Replaces a number of characters

Replaces a single digit

For example, the criterion A* in a First Name field would include any first name beginning with the letter A, such as Anne, Al, or Adam. The criterion A? would only include the name Al, not Anne nor Adam.

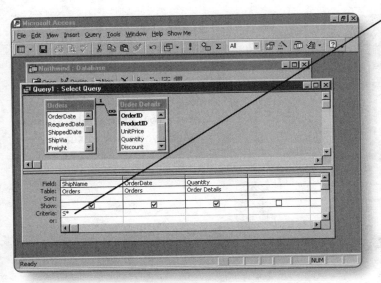

To specify a wildcard pattern, enter the pattern in the Criteria row of the field column in which you want to search.

Specifying Eliminations

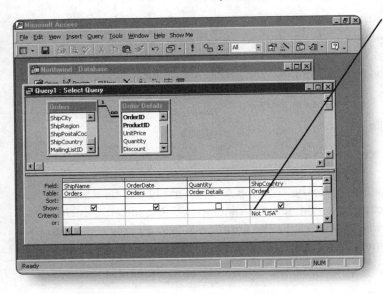

Sometimes you want to tell the query what not to display. For example, you might want to view all employees who are *not* residents of the USA. To specify eliminations, enter Not followed by the elimination term such as "Not USA."

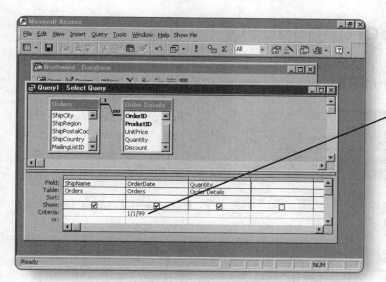

Specifying Dates

You can also specify dates in the Criteria row.

You can enter an exact date, such as 1/1/99, or you can use wildcard operators to specify an entire year. For example, */*/99 would find all dates in 1999.

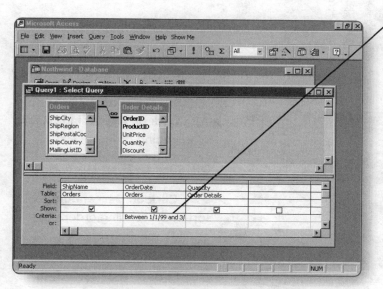

To specify more exact dates, you can use the Between...And operator. For example, Between 1/1/99 and 3/31/99 would find all entries including and between these two dates.

Sorting Query Fields

By default, query fields are not sorted. You can, however, sort any fields in either ascending or descending order.

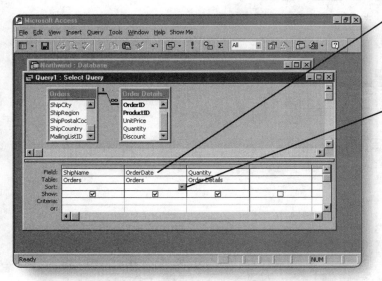

1. Click on the **Sort row** in the field column you want to sort. A down arrow will appear to the right of the field.

2. Click on the **down arrow**. A menu will appear.

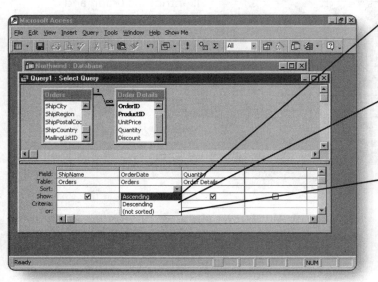

3a. Click on **Ascending** to sort in ascending order.

OR

3b. Click on **Descending** to sort in descending order.

OR

3c. Click on **(not sorted)** to not sort the field.

The sort order will be set based on the instructions in step 3.

Specifying Calculations

Using a query is a convenient way to perform a calculation on a group of records. For example, you may want to know how many orders each salesperson placed last month or the total dollar amount for these orders. You'll use the Total row in the design grid to specify calculation criteria. In Access 2000, you can specify the following calculation types:

- **Group By**. Identifies the group to calculate.

- **Sum**. Totals the values.

- **Avg**. Averages the values.

- **Min**. Finds the minimum value.

- **Max**. Finds the maximum value.

- **Count**. Counts the number of values.

- **StDev**. Calculates the standard deviation of the values.

- **Var**. Calculates the variance of the values.

- **First**. Finds the first field value.

- **Last**. Finds the last field value.

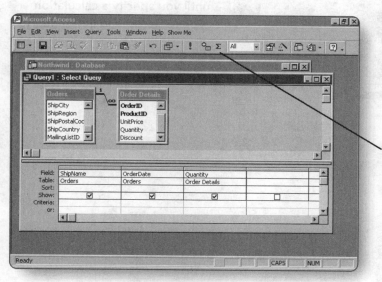

- **Expression**. Creates a calculated field through an expression.

- **Where**. Indicates criteria for a field not included in the query.

1. Click on the **Totals button** on the Toolbar. The Total row will appear in the design grid.

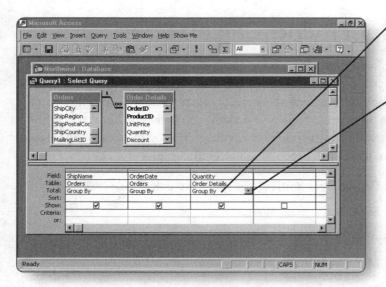

2. **Click** on the **Total row** for the first field whose calculation type you want to specify.

3. **Click** on the **down arrow** to the right of the field. A menu will appear.

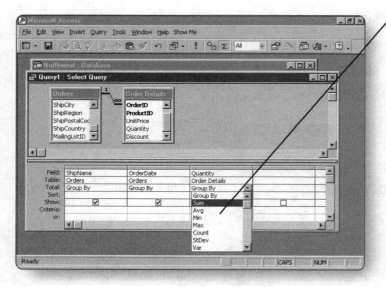

4. **Click** on the **calculation type** you want to apply to that field.

5. **Repeat steps 2** through **4** until you specify a calculation type for each field in the query.

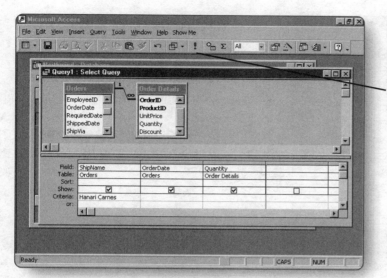

Viewing Query Results

Click on the Run button to view the query results.

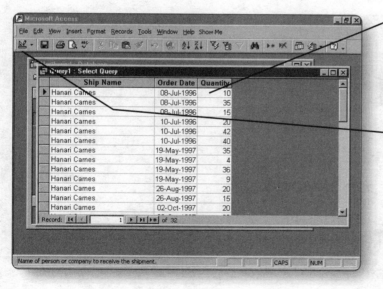

The query displays in Datasheet View. If the results aren't as you intended, you can return to Design View to make further modifications.

To return to Design View, click on the View button.

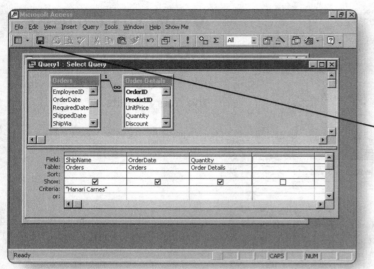

Saving a Query

Once you finish your query and verify that the results are what you want, you can save it.

1. Click on the **Save button**. The Save As dialog box will open.

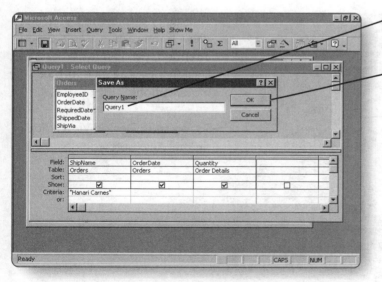

2. Enter a **name for the query** in the Query Name text box.

3. Click on **OK**. The query will be saved.

Part VI Review Questions

1. Which wizard helps you create a basic select query? *See "Starting the Simple Query Wizard" in Chapter 18*

2. What options does a summary query offer? *See "Creating a Summary Query" in Chapter 18*

3. What are the two ways you can open a finished query? *See "Finishing the Query" in Chapter 18*

4. How do you create a query that summarizes information in a spreadsheet format? *See "Starting the Crosstab Query Wizard" in Chapter 19*

5. How many fields can you select as row headings in a crosstab query? *See "Selecting Row Heading Fields" in Chapter 19*

6. How many different summary methods do crosstab queries provide? *See "Selecting a Summary Method" in Chapter 19*

7. In which view can you create a query from scratch? *See "Starting a Query in Design View" in Chapter 20*

8. How do you use the design grid in creating a query? *See "Selecting a Table or Query" in Chapter 20*

9. How can you narrow your query to include or exclude specific information? *See "Specifying Criteria" in Chapter 20*

10. Where can you set calculation criteria in a query? *See "Specifying Calculations" in Chapter 20*

PART VII

Working with Reports

21

Creating an AutoReport

You can simply and easily create basic reports using the AutoReport feature. Using AutoReport, you can automatically create both columnar and tabular reports based on a selected table or query. In this chapter, you'll learn how to:

- Create a Columnar AutoReport
- Create a Tabular AutoReport
- Save and close a report

Creating a Columnar AutoReport

You can automatically create a columnar report based on a selected table or query using the AutoReport feature. In a columnar report, one record at a time will appear on the page, in a vertical format. A columnar report follows the same format as a columnar form.

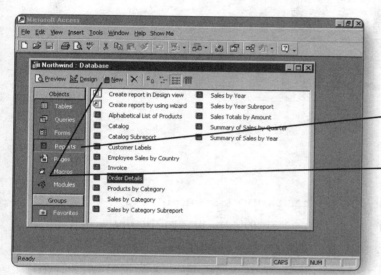

1. **Click** on the **Reports button** in the main database window.

2. **Click** on **New**. The New Report dialog box will open.

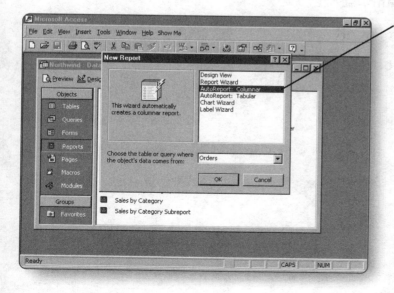

3. **Click** on the **AutoReport: Columnar** option.

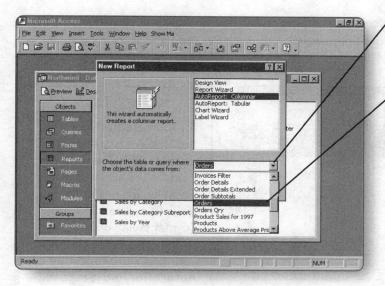

4. Click on the **down arrow** next to the list box. A menu will appear.

5. Click on the **table** on which you want to base your report. The table you choose will appear in the list box.

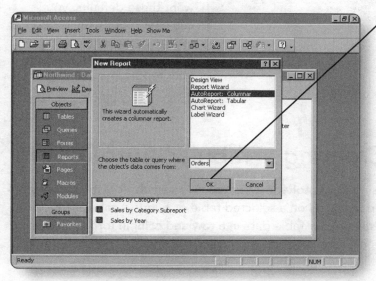

6. Click on **OK**.

A columnar report based on the table you chose will appear in Print Preview. You can print this report as is, or modify its design.

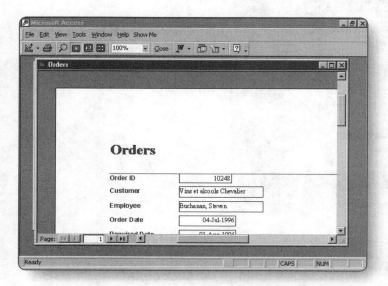

NOTE

A report created using AutoReport has several defaults. It includes all fields in the table or query on which it's based. It defaults to the last Auto-Format style you used or to the Bold format if this is your first AutoReport or AutoForm. And it automatically displays in portrait orientation. If you don't want these defaults, you can later modify the report design or you can use the Report Wizard to create your report instead.

Creating a Tabular AutoReport

Using the AutoReport feature, you can also create a tabular report based on a selected table or query. A tabular report displays your table data in a row and column format. Tabular reports are very similar to tabular forms.

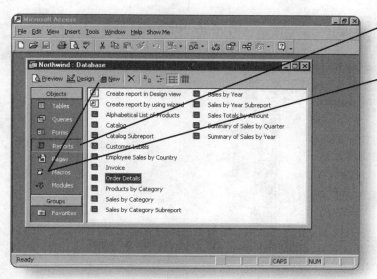

1. **Click** on the **Reports tab** in the main database window.

2. **Click** on **New**. The New Report dialog box will open.

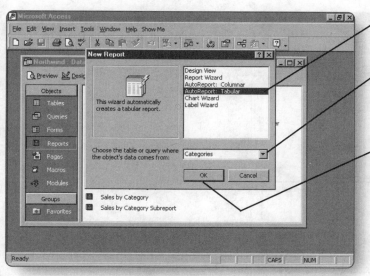

3. **Click** on the **AutoReport: Tabular** option.

4. **Click** on the **down arrow** next to the list box. A menu will appear.

5. **Click** on the **table** you want. The table will appear in the list box.

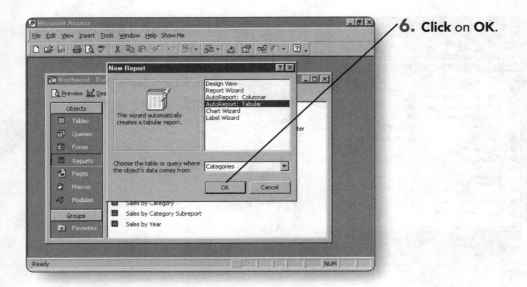

6. Click on **OK**.

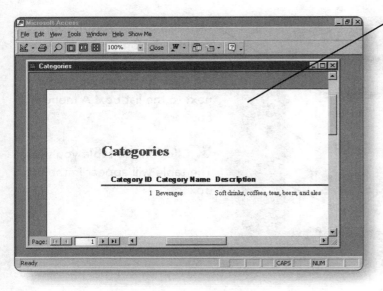

A tabular report based on this table will appear in Print Preview.

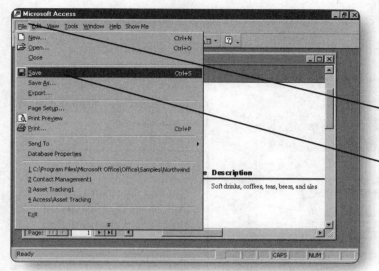

Saving a Report

After you create a report, you'll want to save it.

1. Click on **File**. The File menu will appear.

2. Click on **Save**. The Save As dialog box will open.

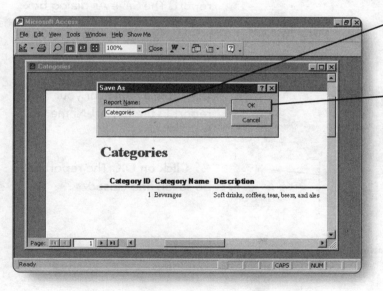

3. Enter a **name** for your report in the Report Name text box.

4. Click on **OK**. The Save As dialog box will close and your report will be saved, but will remain open.

Saving and Closing a Report

You can also save and close a report simultaneously.

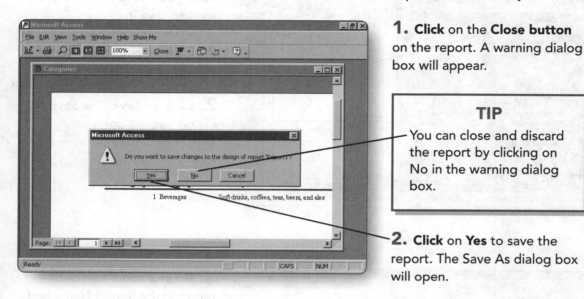

1. Click on the **Close button** on the report. A warning dialog box will appear.

TIP

You can close and discard the report by clicking on No in the warning dialog box.

2. Click on **Yes** to save the report. The Save As dialog box will open.

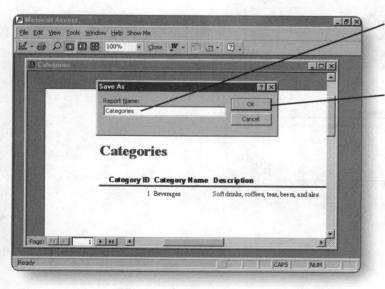

3. Enter a **name** for your report in the Report Name text box.

4. Click on **OK**. The report will be saved and closed.

22

Creating a Report with the Report Wizard

Using the Report Wizard, you can create a report in a matter of minutes and still have the opportunity to specify many of your own parameters. The Report Wizard lets you set grouping, sorting, and summary options as well as choose your own style and layouts. In this chapter, you'll learn how to:

- Start the Report Wizard
- Select fields
- Create groupings and sort orders
- Specify summary options
- Specify the report layout and style
- Finish the report

Starting the Report Wizard

The Report Wizard offers step-by-step guidance on creating detailed reports, including those that contain fields from more than one table or query.

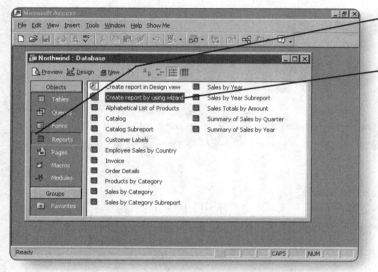

1. **Click** on the **Reports button** in the main database window.

2. **Double-click** on **Create report by using wizard** within the database window. The Report Wizard will open.

Selecting Fields

In the second step, you choose the specific fields to place in your report, including the table or query in which they are located.

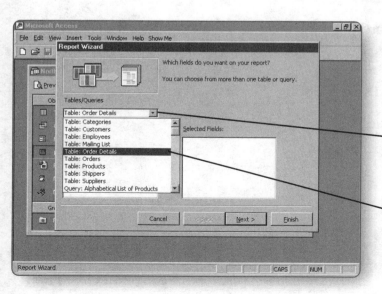

1. **Click** on the **down arrow** to the right of the Tables/Queries list box. A menu will appear.

2. **Click** on the **table** or **query** from which you want to select your report fields. The table or query will appear in the list box.

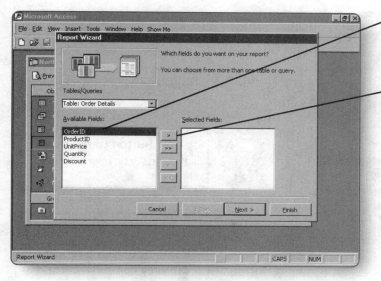

3. Choose the **first field** you want to include in your report from the Available Fields list.

4. Click on the **right arrow button**. The field will move to the Selected Fields scroll box.

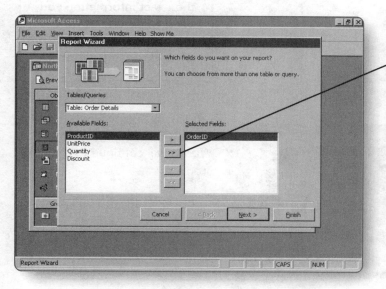

TIP

Click on the double right arrow button to include all available fields in your report.

5. Repeat steps 1 through **4** until you select all the fields you want to include in your report.

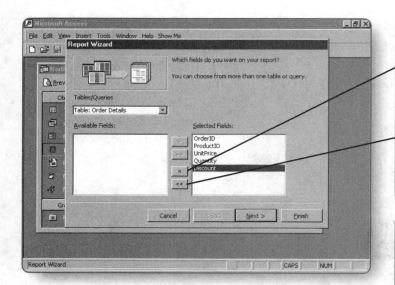

TIP

Click on the left arrow button to remove the selected field from the report.

Click on the double left arrow button to remove all fields from your report.

NOTE

Remember that a report can only contain a certain number of fields on one page. Consider carefully the exact information you need to include as well as the width of each field when designing a report.

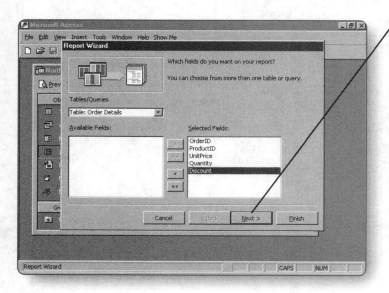

6. Click on **Next**. The Report Wizard will continue to the next step.

Creating Groupings

You can create report groupings based on one or several fields.

1. Click on the **field** on which you want to group from the list of available fields.

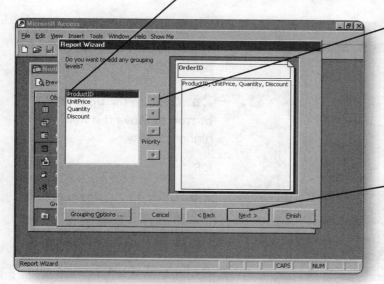

2. Click on the **right arrow button**. The selected field will be displayed in blue bold text in the preview box to the right.

3. Repeat steps 1 and **2** until you select all the fields on which you want to group.

4. Click on **Next** to continue.

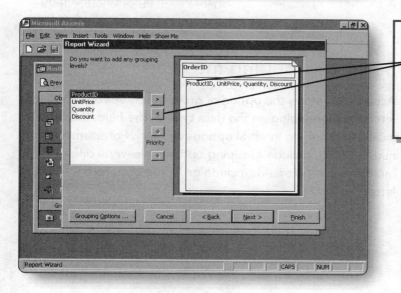

TIP

To remove a field grouping, click on the field name, then click on the left arrow button.

Changing the Grouping Priority

In the preview window, the grouping level fields are displayed in blue bold text and are listed in order of grouping priority, with each subsequent level slightly indented. The order is based on the order in which you specify grouping levels, but you can easily change it.

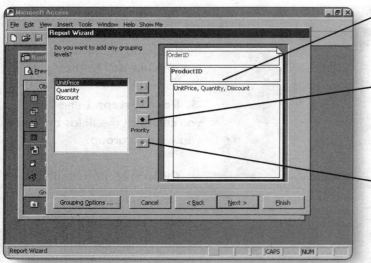

1. Click on the **grouping field** in the preview box whose priority you want to change.

2a. Click on the **up arrow button** to move this field to a higher priority.

OR

2b. Click on the **down arrow button** to move this field to a lower priority.

3. Repeat steps 1 and **2** until you've changed the grouping priorities to the desired order.

Setting Grouping Intervals

Access also offers the option of grouping by specified intervals. Depending on the data type of the field, the available grouping interval options will vary. For example, number fields include grouping options in several different multiples and text fields include grouping options based on letter.

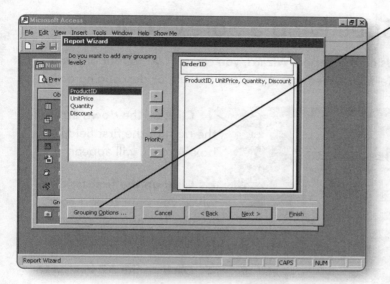

1. Click on the **Grouping Options button**. The Grouping Intervals dialog box will open.

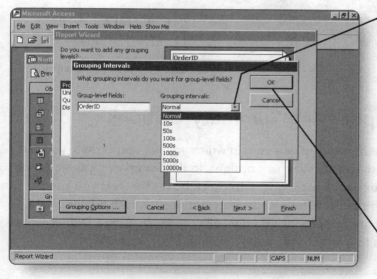

2. Click on the **down arrow** to the right of the Grouping intervals list box. A menu will appear.

3. Click on the **interval** you want. The interval you chose will appear in the list box.

4. Repeat step 2 until you set all grouping intervals.

5. Click on **OK**.

TIP

Grouping intervals are only available for fields on which you've already specified a grouping level.

Specifying a Sort Order

Using the Report Wizard, you can sort up to four different fields in either ascending (the default) or descending order.

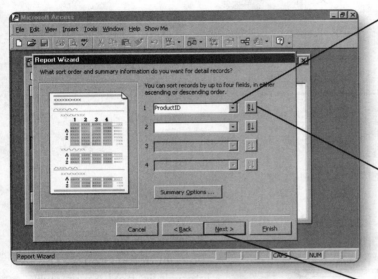

1. **Click** on the **down arrow** to the right of the first field list box. A menu will appear.

2. **Click on the first field** on which you want to sort your report. The ascending sort order will be automatically applied.

3. **Click** on the **AZ button** to change the sort order to descending, if desired.

4. **Repeat steps 1, 2, and 3** until you select all sort orders.

5. **Click** on **Next** to continue.

Specifying Summary Options

In the same wizard step in which you set sort orders, you can also specify summary options. In the Summary Options dialog box, you'll see a grid with check boxes that lets you specify up to four different summary options for each numeric field. These options include the ability to summarize a field as well as to display its average, minimum, or maximum.

CAUTION

The Summary Options button won't appear in this step if your report doesn't include any numeric fields.

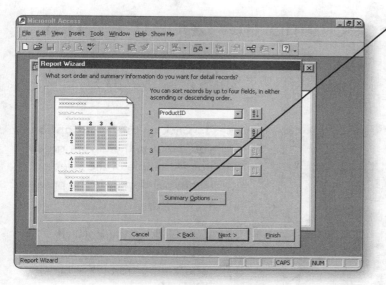

1. Click on the **Summary Options button**. The Summary Options dialog box will open.

2. Click on the **check box** for each field and summary option combination you want to include in your report.

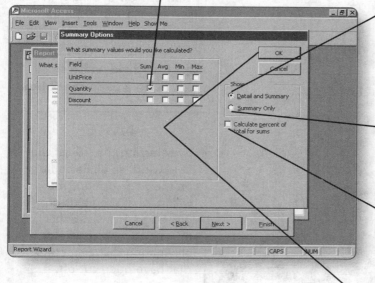

3a. Click on the **Detail and Summary option button** to display both detail and summary information in your report.

OR

3b. Click on the **Summary Only option button** to display just the summary information in the report.

4. Click on the **Calculate percent of total for sums check box** to display the percentage of the total this amount represents.

5. Click on **OK**.

Specifying the Report Layout

Next, you can choose the report layout you prefer from a selection of several different layouts. You can also set your report's orientation.

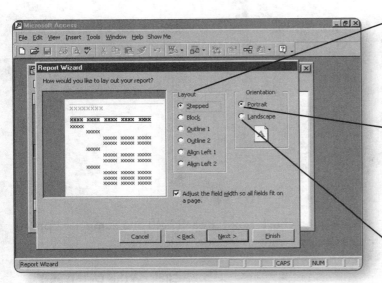

1. **Click** on the **layout option** you prefer in the Layout group box. A sample of the selected layout will display in the preview box.

2a. **Click** on the **Portrait option button** to display your report in portrait (8½ x 11) orientation.

OR

2b. **Click** on the **Landscape option button** to display in landscape (11 x 8½) orientation.

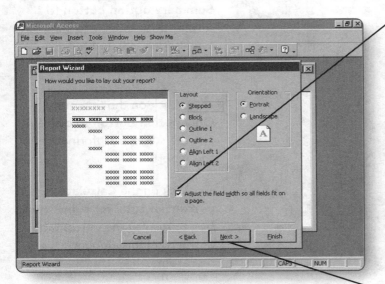

3. If you need to, **click** on the **Adjust the field width so all fields fit on a page check box.**

NOTE

By selecting the Adjust the field width so all fields fit on the page option, you will fit all of the fields on one page. However, this may truncate some fields, eliminating the characters that have been cut off.

4. **Click** on **Next** to continue.

Choosing a Report Style

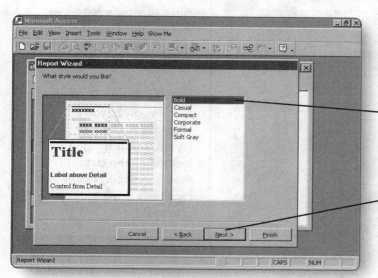

Access includes six predefined report styles, both casual and formal, from which you can choose.

1. Choose the **report style** you prefer from the list. A sample of the selected style will appear in the preview box.

2. Click on **Next** to continue.

Finishing the Report

In the final step of the Report Wizard, you'll create a report title and select the view you want to use when opening the report for the first time.

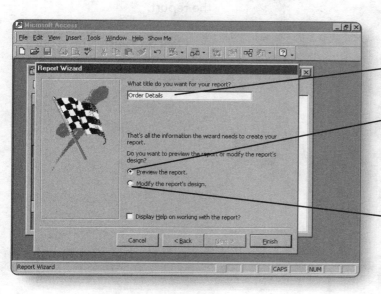

1. Enter a **name** for your report in the text box.

2a. Click on the **Preview the report option button** to open the report in Print Preview.

OR

2b. Click on the **Modify the report's design option button** to open the report in Design View.

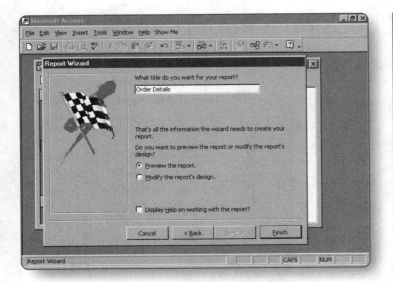

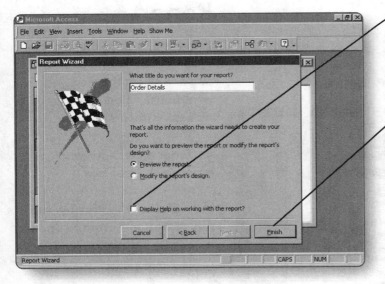

3. Click on the **Display Help on working with the report check box** if you want to display a help window when you open the report.

4. Click on **Finish**. The report will open based on your instructions in step 2.

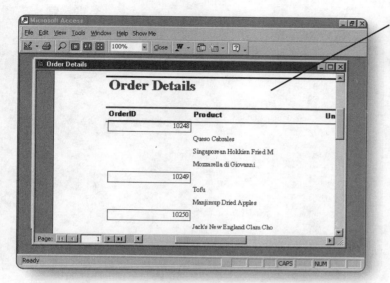

If you open your report in Print Preview, you'll see exactly how it will look on paper.

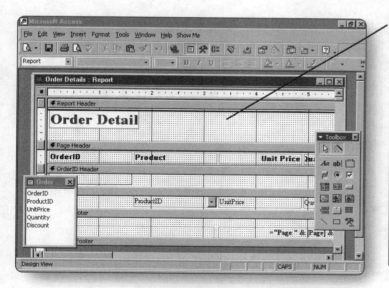

If your final report isn't exactly what you want, you can customize it in Design View.

TIP

If you decide you want to start over again after creating a report, you can delete it by selecting it in the main database window and pressing the Delete key.

23

Changing a Report's Appearance

Once you create a report, you may want to change its default style or customize its formatting in other ways. In this chapter, you will learn how to:

- Open a report in Design View
- Change a report's format
- Modify fonts
- Bold, italicize, and underline
- Set alignment

Opening a Report in Design View

You can open an existing report in Design View to modify its design.

1. Click on the **Reports button** in the main database window.

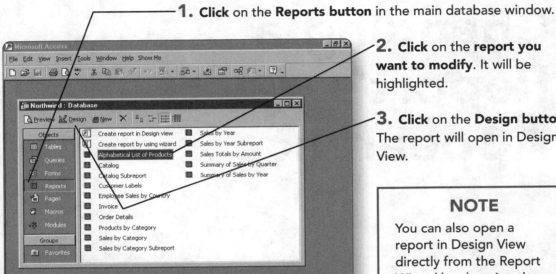

2. Click on the **report you want to modify**. It will be highlighted.

3. Click on the **Design button**. The report will open in Design View.

NOTE

You can also open a report in Design View directly from the Report Wizard by choosing the Modify the report's design option button on the final wizard step.

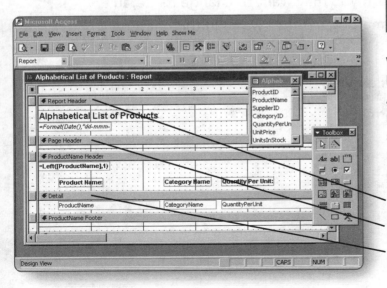

When you look at a report in Design View, you'll see that an Access report consists of a number of controls placed in specific report sections. Each report includes the following sections:

- Report Header
- Page Header
- Detail

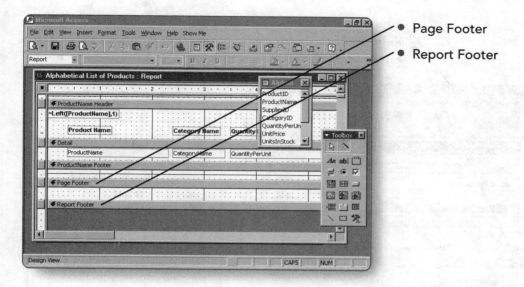

● Page Footer

● Report Footer

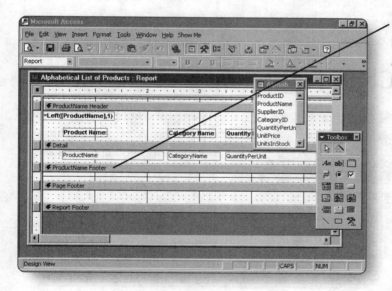

Reports can also include group headers and footers if you applied groupings to the reports.

Report controls are objects such as labels or text boxes. The Report Wizard and AutoReport features automatically create report sections and place controls in the appropriate location. You can also create or modify report controls manually.

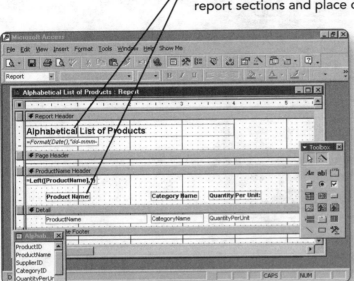

TIP

Creating report controls or making major modifications to them is an advanced feature of Access. If you're a novice user, it's usually easier to create a new report based on new report specifications than it is to make extensive modifications.

Changing a Report's Format

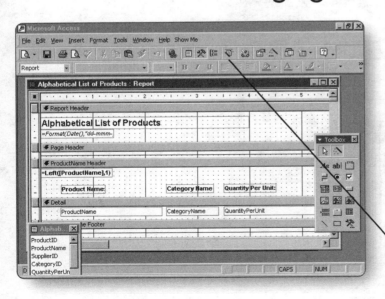

When you create a report using the Report Wizard or AutoReport feature, you choose a style or AutoFormat to apply. This format uses predefined colors, borders, fonts, and font sizes designed to look good together and convey a specific image. If you don't like the AutoFormat you originally chose for your report, you can change it.

1. Click on the **AutoFormat button**. The AutoFormat dialog box will open with the current format highlighted.

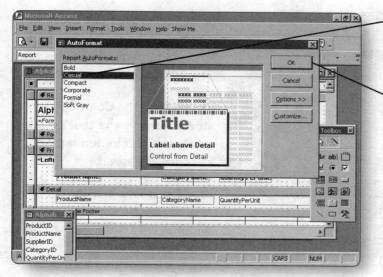

2. Click on a **new report format** in the Report AutoFormats list.

3. Click on **OK** to apply the new format.

Selecting Specific Formatting Options

By default, an AutoFormat applies to all the fonts, colors, and borders on a report. You can use the Options button in the AutoFormat dialog box to apply changes only to specific parts of the report.

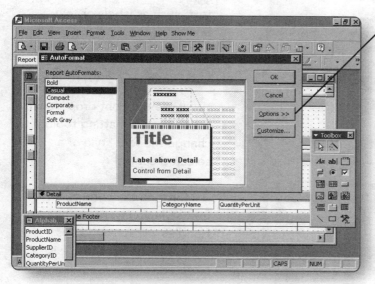

1. Click on the **Options button**. The AutoFormat dialog box will extend to include the Attributes to Apply group box. All three attributes are selected by default.

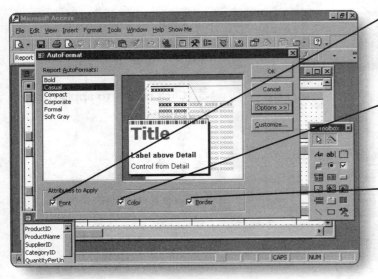

2. Click on the **Font check box** to remove the check mark and prevent formatting changes to fonts, if desired.

3. Click on the **Color check box** to remove the check mark and prevent color formatting changes, if desired.

4. Click on the **Border check box** to remove the check mark and prevent border formatting changes, if desired.

CAUTION

Remember that Access AutoFormats and styles were designed to look good together. If you make too many font changes, your report may look muddled or hard to read.

Changing Fonts

You can also change only the fonts in your report rather than the entire format or style. You can change the fonts of all report controls that contain text, such as labels or text boxes.

Changing Font Style

You'll use the Font drop-down list on the Formatting toolbar to change the font style of a selected control.

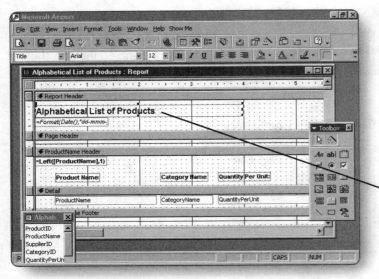

1. Click on the **control** whose font style you want to change. Handles will surround this control to indicate that it is selected.

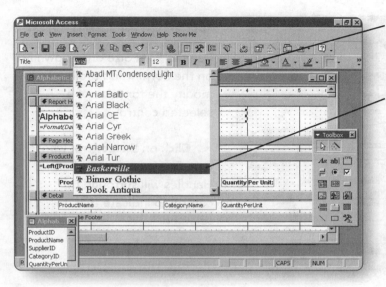

2. Click on the **down arrow** to the right of the Font drop-down list. A menu will appear.

3. Click on a **new font**.

TIP

The fonts that display from the Font drop-down list depend on the fonts you have installed on your computer.

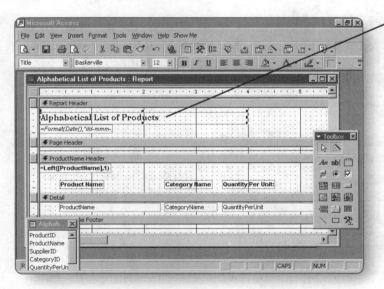

The new font style will appear in your report.

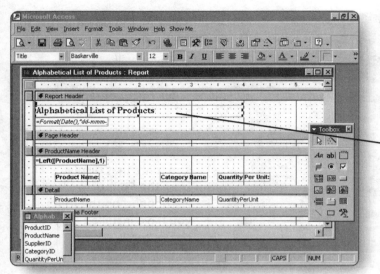

Changing Font Size

Use the Font Size drop-down list on the Formatting toolbar to modify the font size of a selected control.

1. Click on the **control** whose font size you want to change. Handles will surround this control to indicate that it is selected.

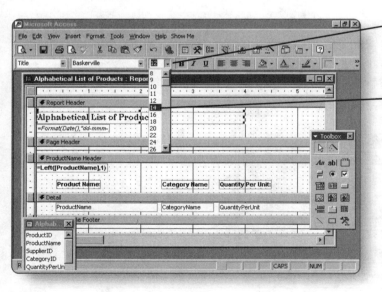

2. Click on the **down arrow** to the right of the Font Size drop-down list. A menu will appear.

3. Click on a **new font size**.

NOTE
You can choose font sizes from 8 to 72 points.

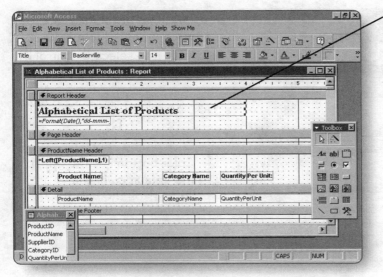

The text will appear in the new font size.

Changing Font Color

You'll use the Font/Fore Color button on the Formatting toolbar to change font color in a report.

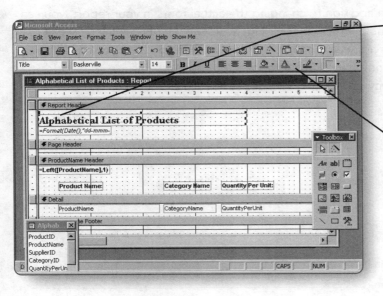

1. Click on the **control** whose font color you want to modify. Handles will surround this control to indicate that it is selected.

2. Click on the **down arrow** to the right of the Font/Fore Color button. The font color palette will open.

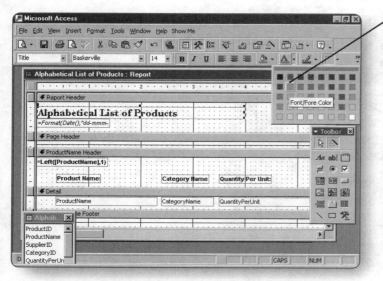

3. Click on the **color** you want to apply from the font color palette. The selected control will display in the new font color.

TIP

Click on the Font/Fore Color button itself to apply the default color that appears on the button.

Bolding, Italicizing, and Underlining

In addition to changing the actual fonts in your report, you can modify them by bolding, italicizing, and underlining. These features are particularly useful when you want to emphasize something in your report. You can bold, italicize, and underline any control that includes text, such as a label or text box.

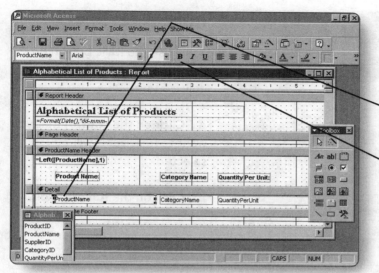

Bolding Text

You'll use the Bold button on the Formatting toolbar to bold text.

1. Click on the **control** that you want to bold. It will be selected.

2. Click on the **Bold button**.

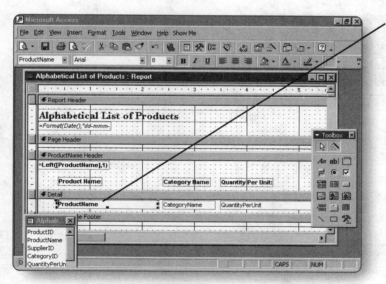

The text will appear bolded.

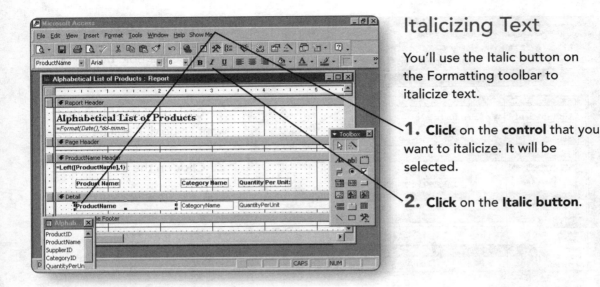

Italicizing Text

You'll use the Italic button on the Formatting toolbar to italicize text.

1. Click on the **control** that you want to italicize. It will be selected.

2. Click on the **Italic button**.

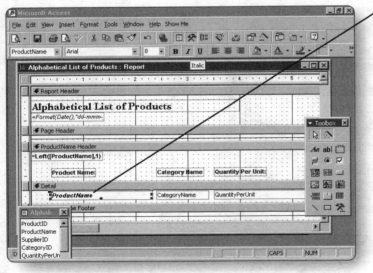

The text will be italicized.

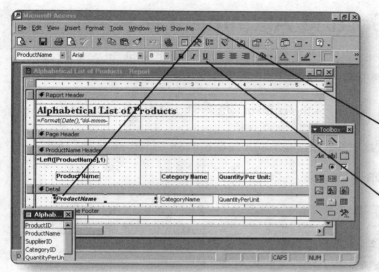

Underlining Text

You'll use the Underline button on the Formatting toolbar to underline text.

1. **Click** on the **control** that you want to underline. It will be selected.

2. **Click** on the **Underline button**.

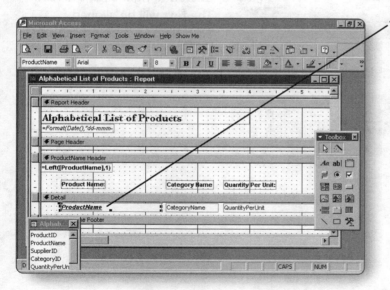

The text will be underlined.

Setting Alignment

You can set left, center, and right alignment on your Access reports using buttons on the Formatting toolbar.

1. **Click** on the **control** whose alignment you want to change.

2a. **Click** on the **Align Left button** to left align the text.

OR

2b. **Click** on the **Center button** to center selected text.

OR

2c. **Click** on the **Align Right button** to right align the text. The text will be aligned according to your instructions in step 2.

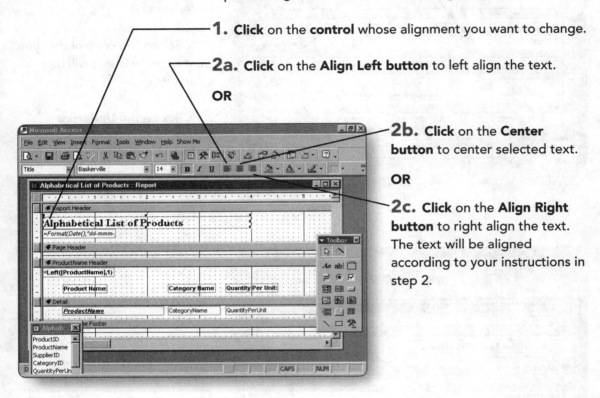

24

Printing Reports

You can print a report with the click of a button in Access, but the program also offers options for specifying exact report parameters as well. In this chapter, you'll learn how to:

● Open a report in Print Preview

● Print a default report

● Print a report with specific options

Opening a Report in Print Preview

You can open an existing report in Print Preview to see how it will look before you print.

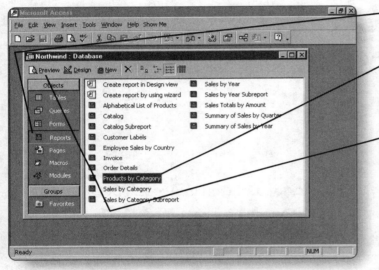

1. Click on the **Reports button** in the main database window.

2. Click on the **report** you want to preview. It will be highlighted.

3. Click on the **Preview button**. The report will open in Print Preview.

NOTE

You can also open a report in Print Preview directly from the Report Wizard by choosing the Preview the Report option button on the final wizard step.

TIP

To change the default page orientation (portrait or landscape) before you print, choose File, Page Setup and select either the Portrait or Landscape option button on the Page tab of the Page Setup dialog box.

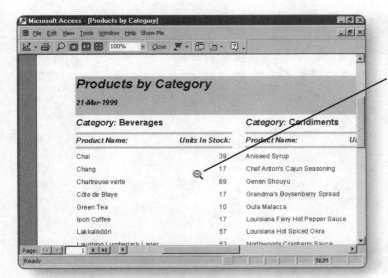

Zooming In on a Report

In Print Preview, the mouse pointer becomes a magnifying glass that you can use to zoom in and out of a specific area of the report for more detail. When you open a report, you will zoom in to the upper left corner at 100%.

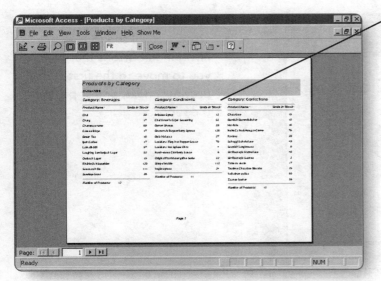

To display a full-page view, click anywhere on the report.

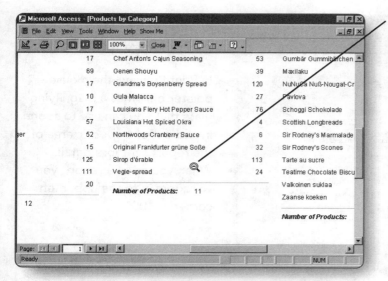

To view a particular area in more detail, click on that part of the report.

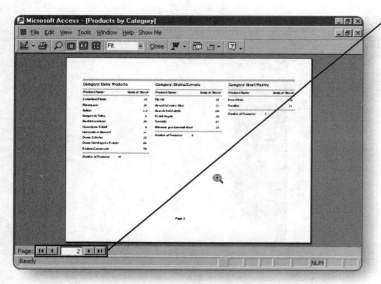

In the lower left portion of the screen, you'll see four navigation buttons that enable you to move to the first, previous, next, or last page in the report.

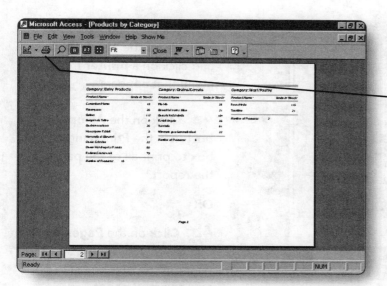

Printing a Default Report

You can quickly and easily print a report using the default settings by clicking on the Print button in Print Preview.

NOTE

The Access printing default is set to print one copy of all pages of a report using the default printer you specified in Windows.

Printing a Report with Specific Options

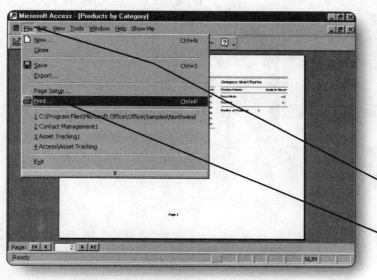

When you print a report, you may want to set options such as the specific pages and number of copies to print. If you have the capability to print to more than one printer, you'll want to be sure you specify the appropriate printer.

1. Click on **File**. The File menu will appear.

2. Click on **Print**. The Print dialog box will open.

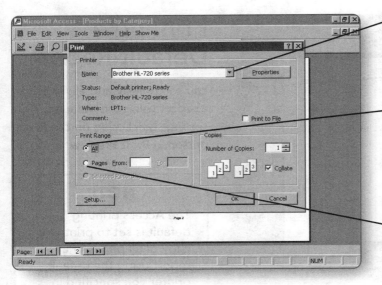

3. Click on the **down arrow** to the right of the Name list box and click on a **printer** from the menu that appears.

4a. Click on the **All option button** in the Print Range group box to print all of the pages in the report.

OR

4b. Click on the **Pages option button,** then enter the specific pages in the text boxes to print only selected pages.

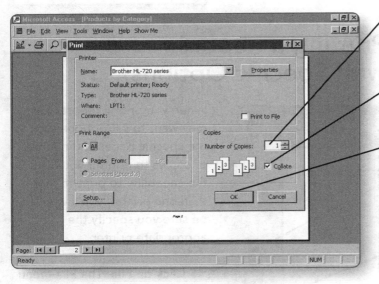

5. Choose the **number of copies** to print from the Copies scroll box.

6. Click on the **Collate check box** to collate multiple copies.

7. Click on **OK**. The report will print.

Setting Up Margins

You can also specify changes in the margins through the Print dialog box. Default margin settings are one inch on all sides—top, bottom, left, and right. These defaults work well in most circumstances, but if your report won't fit on a page, you may want to adjust the margins.

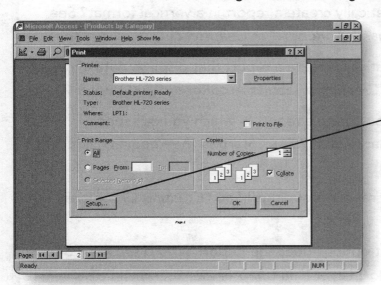

1. Click on the **Setup button**. The Page Setup dialog box will open.

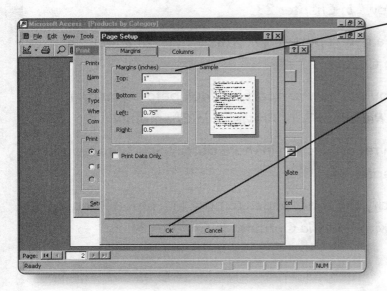

2. Enter the **desired margins** in the Margins (inches) text boxes.

3. Click on **OK**. You will return to the Print dialog box.

Part VII Review Questions

1. How do you automatically create a report in a vertical format? *See "Creating a Columnar AutoReport" in Chapter 21*

2. How do you automatically create a report that displays data in rows and columns? *See "Creating a Tabular AutoReport" in Chapter 21*

3. Which wizard lets you create a report in which you can specify many of your own parameters? *See "Starting the Report Wizard" in Chapter 22*

4. How do you specify report groupings? *See "Creating Groupings" in Chapter 22*

5. What kinds of layout options does the Report Wizard provide? *See "Specifying the Report Layout" in Chapter 22*

6. In which view can you modify a report's design? *See "Opening a Report in Design View" in Chapter 23*

7. How can you apply a new report AutoFormat? *See "Changing a Report's Format" in Chapter 23*

8. In which view can you see how a report will look before you print it? *See "Opening a Report in Print Preview" in Chapter 24*

9. How can you view a report section in more detail? *See "Zooming In on a Report" in Chapter 24*

10. Where can you specify the exact pages to print in a report? *See "Printing a Report with Specific Options" in Chapter 24*

PART VIII

Working with the Web

25

Adding Hyperlinks

Access includes the powerful ability to link data in tables and forms to documents on the Internet, your company's network, or your own computer hard drive through the use of *hyperlinks*. In this chapter, you will learn how to:

- Add hyperlinks to a table in Design View
- Add a hyperlink column in Datasheet View
- Enter hyperlinks in tables
- Test your hyperlinks
- Add a hyperlink label to a form

Adding Hyperlinks to a Table in Design View

You can include hyperlinks to the following:

● Documents on the Internet, such as a World Wide Web page.

● Documents on your company network's intranet site (internal Internet).

● Documents on your own computer's hard drive, such as other Office 2000 files.

For example, in a table that stores customer information, you might want to include a field that links to each customer's Web site. You can add a hyperlink field to a table in Design View.

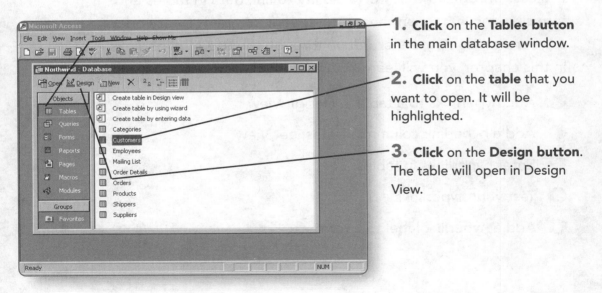

1. Click on the **Tables button** in the main database window.

2. Click on the **table** that you want to open. It will be highlighted.

3. Click on the **Design button**. The table will open in Design View.

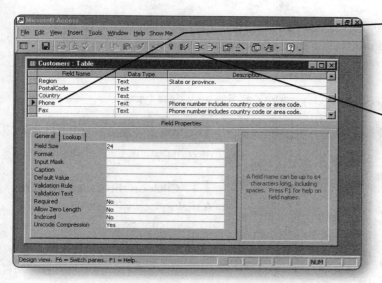

4. Click on the **row beneath where you want to add a field**. An arrow will appear in the field selector column.

5. Click on the **Insert Rows button**. A blank row will be added.

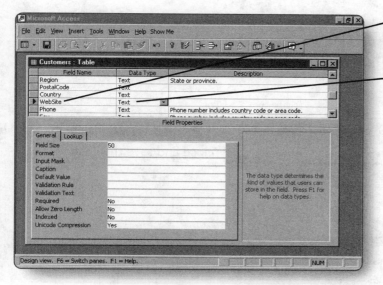

6. Enter the **name for the new field** in the Field Name column.

7. Press the **Tab key** to move to the Data Type column.

8. Click on the **down arrow** to the left of the Data Type column in the field row whose data type you want to change. A menu will appear.

9. Click on **Hyperlink** as the new data type.

10. Enter a **description** of the new hyperlink field, if desired.

11. Click on the **Close button**. A dialog box will ask if you want to save changes.

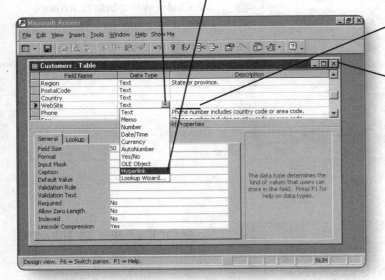

12. Click on **Yes**. The table will close and save the changes.

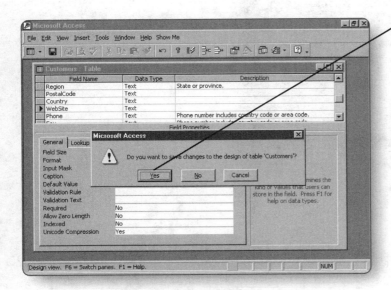

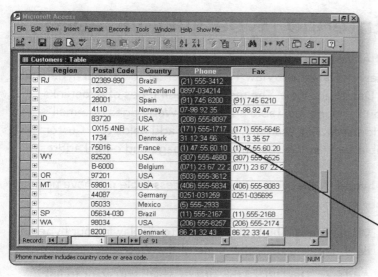

Adding Hyperlink Columns in Datasheet View

If you are already in Datasheet View, you can add a hyperlink column directly to the table datasheet.

1. Select the **field column** to the right of where you want to insert the hyperlink column.

2. Click on **Insert**. The Insert menu will appear.

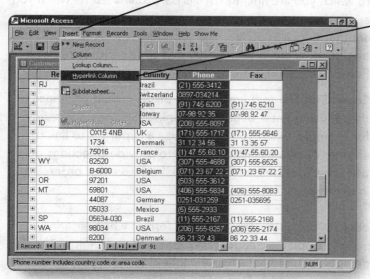

3. Click on **Hyperlink Column**. A hyperlink field will be inserted to the left of the selected column.

When you save the changes, the new field will automatically be saved with the Hyperlink data type.

NOTE

If you use this shortcut method to add a hyperlink column, you must rename the column, then set any additional properties in Design View.

Entering Hyperlinks in Tables

After you add a hyperlink field to a table—either in Design View or Datasheet View—you can enter the actual hyperlinks in Datasheet View. The most common types of hyperlinks you'll include in a table are links to Web pages or e-mail addresses. For example, you could add fields to a Customers table that list the customer's Web page and e-mail address.

A hyperlink that you store in an Access table can have up to four parts:

- **Display text**. The text you want to display in your hyperlink field. This is usually the name of the Web site.

- **Address**. The URL of the site to which you want to link. Http://www.microsoft.com is an example of an address.

> **NOTE**
>
> URL refers to Uniform Resource Locator, the address of the Internet document, Web page, or object to which you want to link. It includes the protocol, such as http, as well the exact address location.

- **Subaddress**. The exact location in the document or page to which you are linking. This is particularly useful when you are linking to another document on your computer, such as another Office 2000 file. The subaddress could be a bookmark name in Word 2000 or a slide number in PowerPoint 2000, for example.

- **ScreenTip**. The text you want to display when you place the mouse pointer over a hyperlink. A ScreenTip is handy, for example, when you want to use a hyperlink to link to another Access object and need to provide directions on what the link does, such as "Click here to enter order information."

Access 2000 requires the following format when entering a hyperlink: displaytext#address#subaddress#screentip. The address is required for a hyperlink field to work properly; the display text, subaddress, and ScreenTip are optional.

To enter a hyperlink in a table, you need to open it in Datasheet View.

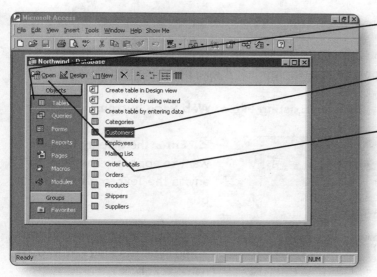

1. **Click** on the **Tables button** in the main database window.

2. **Click** on the **table you want to open**. It will be highlighted.

3. **Click** on the **Open button**. The table will open in Datasheet View.

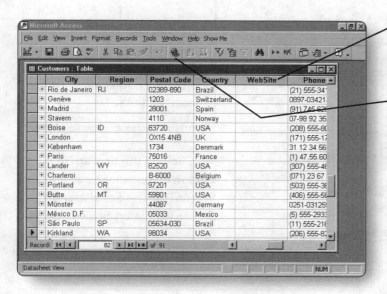

4. **Press** the **Tab key** to move to the **field** in which you want to enter the hyperlink.

5. **Click** on the **Insert Hyperlink button**. The Insert Hyperlink dialog box will open. In this dialog box, you can create several types of hyperlinks, including those to existing Web pages or e-mail addresses, two of the most common types of hyperlinks in tables.

Linking to a Web Page

You can set up a link to an external Web page on the Internet from the Insert Hyperlink dialog box.

1. Click the **Existing File or Web Page button**.

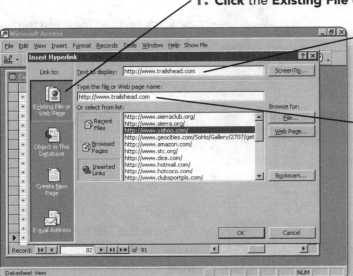

2. Enter the **display text** you want to appear in the field, if any, in the Text to display text box.

3. Enter the **hyperlink address** in the Type the file or Web page name text box.

TIP

You can also select the hyperlink address from the list of recent files, browsed pages, or inserted links.

4. Click on the **ScreenTip button** if you want to add a ScreenTip. The Set Hyperlink ScreenTip dialog box will open.

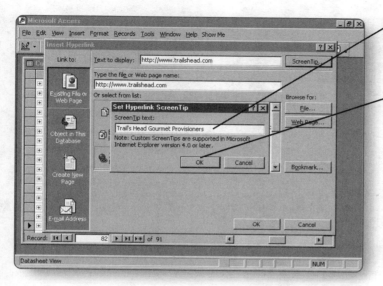

5. Enter the **text** you want to appear as a ScreenTip in the ScreenTip text: text box.

6. Click on **OK** to return to the Insert Hyperlink dialog box.

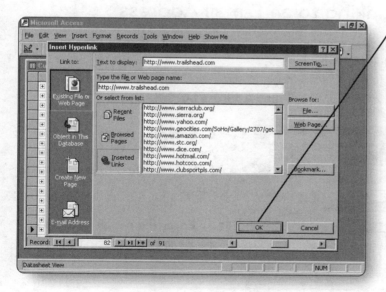

7. Click on **OK**.

NOTE

A hyperlink will display in colored, underlined text. This indicates that when you click on it, it will link you to the designated file or location.

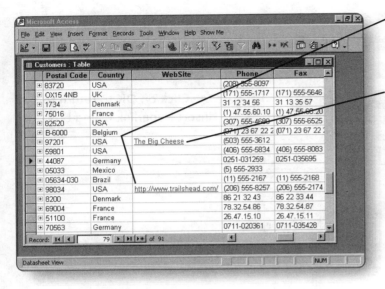

If you enter just a hyperlink address, the address will appear in the hyperlink field.

If you enter display text plus an address, subaddress, or ScreenTip, only the display text will appear.

Linking to an E-mail Address

You can also link to an e-mail address from within the Insert Hyperlink dialog box.

1. Click on the **E-mail Address button**.

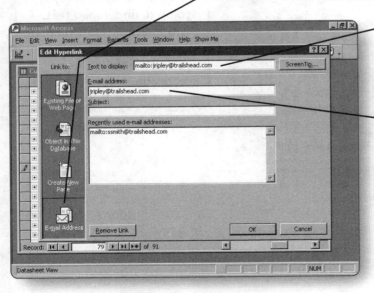

2. Enter the **display text** that you want to appear in the field, if any, in the Text to display text box.

3. Enter the **e-mail address** in the E-mail address text box.

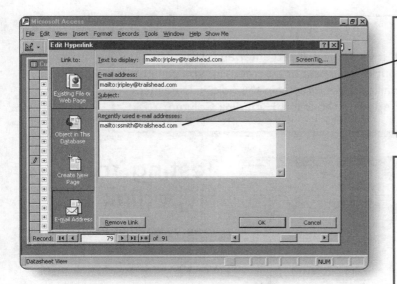

TIP

You can also select an e-mail address from the Recently used e-mail addresses list.

NOTE

As soon as you enter an e-mail address, it is automatically prefaced by the phrase mailto:. This phrase is required to send an e-mail.

4. **Enter** the **information** you would like to automatically appear in the subject of your e-mail message in the Subject text box. This is optional.

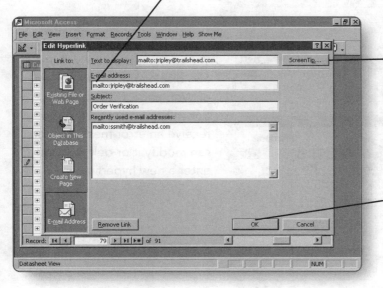

TIP

You can also include a ScreenTip by clicking on the ScreenTip button and entering a ScreenTip in the Set Hyperlink ScreenTip dialog box.

5. **Click** on **OK** to return to Datasheet View.

TIP

As a shortcut, if you only want to enter an e-mail address without display text or a ScreenTip, you can just enter the e-mail address directly in the field in Datasheet View without opening the Insert Hyperlink Column.

Testing Your Hyperlink

To verify whether a hyperlink you've created works properly, you should test it.

To test a hyperlink, click on it.

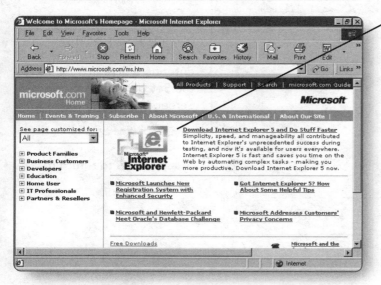

Your default browser will open and display the linked document or Web page. If the hyperlink doesn't open properly or you receive an error message, you can modify it or delete it and enter a new hyperlink.

Adding a Hyperlink Label to a Form

You can also include hyperlink fields in forms. In general, a hyperlink field that exists in a table will appear like any other field in a form. For example, if you have a Customers table that includes hyperlink fields to display the Web page and e-mail addresses of each customer, these fields would appear as a regular field in a form. The only difference would be that they are underlined, which indicates that they are hyperlinks.

You can also add your own hyperlink fields to a form. An example of when you would use this would be if you wanted to provide a link from one Access form to another. In this case, a user could click on the hyperlink in the main form to jump to the other form.

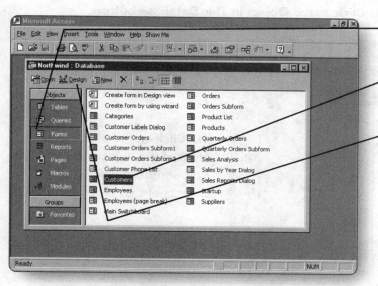

1. **Click** on the **Forms button** in the main database window.

2. **Click** on the **form you want to open**. It will be highlighted.

3. **Click** on the **Design button**. The form will open in Design View.

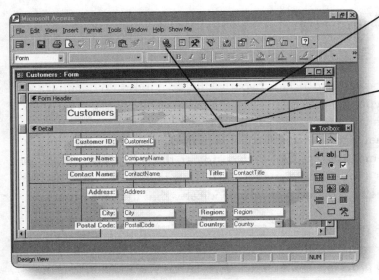

4. Click on the **location on the form** where you want to place the hyperlink.

5. Click on the **Insert Hyperlink button**. The Insert Hyperlink dialog box will open.

6. Click on the **Object in This Database button**.

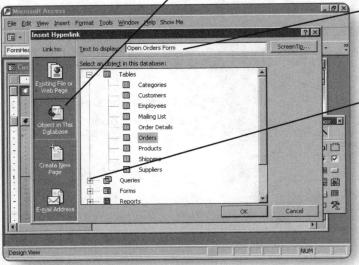

7. Enter the **display text** that you want to appear in the field, if any, in the Text to display text box.

8. Click on the **plus sign** in front of the object type to which you want to link. A list of objects of that type will appear.

9. Click on the **specific object** to which you want to link.

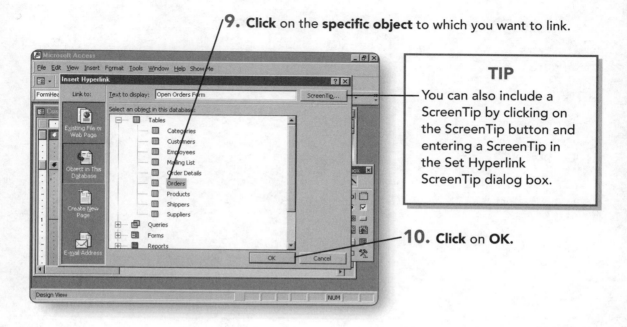

TIP

You can also include a ScreenTip by clicking on the ScreenTip button and entering a ScreenTip in the Set Hyperlink ScreenTip dialog box.

10. Click on **OK**.

Click on the View button to preview the form in Form View. When you click on the hyperlink, you will jump to the other form.

If you created a ScreenTip, the tip will appear when you position the mouse pointer over the link.

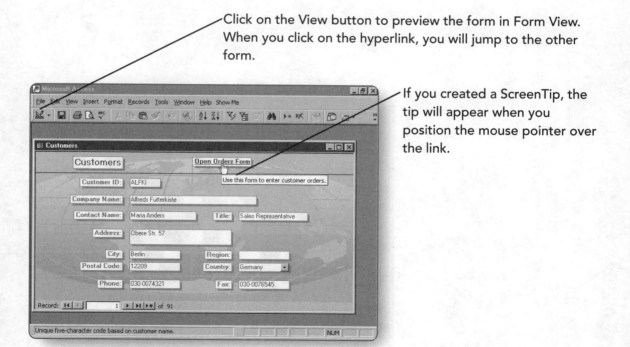

26

Creating Data Access Pages

Access includes an object called a *data access page* that enables users to view and access your Access databases via the Web. Using the AutoPage or Page Wizard features, you can quickly create a page, specify options such as sort order and theme, and then preview your work via a browser. In this chapter, you'll learn how to:

- Understand data access pages
- Create a columnar AutoPage
- Create a data access page with the Page Wizard
- Preview a data access page

Understanding Data Access Pages

A data access page is very similar to a form or report, except that it functions as a Web page. A user can open your data access page from either the Internet or internal company intranet. You can create data access pages to view, analyze, and report on information or to serve as a method of data entry. In the latter case, you could potentially have multiple users updating table information over the Internet. You'll most likely use data access pages if you create multi-user Access databases and already have a Web or intranet site on which to place the pages.

> **CAUTION**
>
> You must have Microsoft Internet Explorer 5 installed on your system to fully make use of the data access page capabilities. If you chose not to install Internet Explorer 5 during your initial installation or have removed it from your system, you can reinstall it from the Office 2000 CD.

Creating a Columnar AutoPage

You can automatically create a columnar page based on a selected table or query using the AutoPage feature. In a columnar page, one record will appear on the page at a time, in a vertical format. A columnar page follows the same format as a columnar form or report.

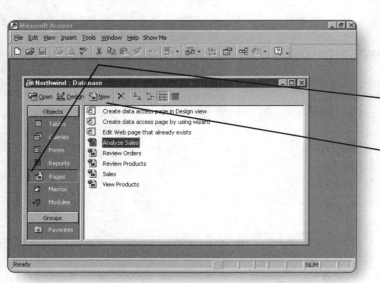

1. Click on the **Pages button** in the main database window.

2. Click on **New**. The New Data Access Page dialog box will open.

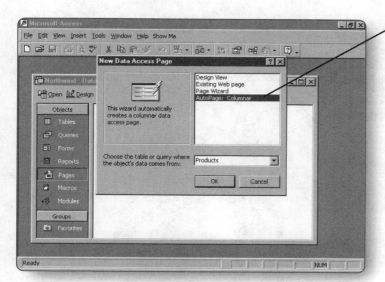

3. Click on the **AutoPage: Columnar** option.

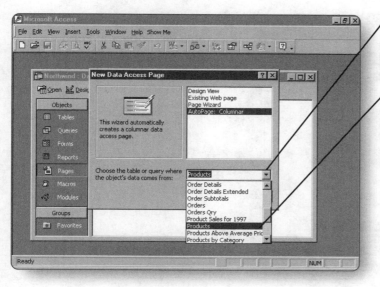

4. Click on the **down arrow** next to the list box. A menu will appear.

5. Click on the **table or query** on which you want to base your page. The table or query will appear in the list box.

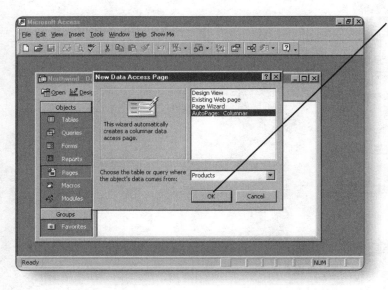

6. Click on **OK**.

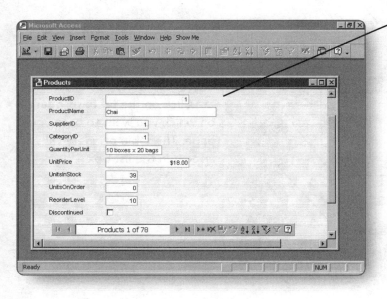

A columnar page based on this table will appear in Page View. You can later modify its design in Design View, if desired.

Creating a Page with the Page Wizard

The Page Wizard offers step-by-step guidance on creating detailed data access pages, including those that contain fields from more than one table or query.

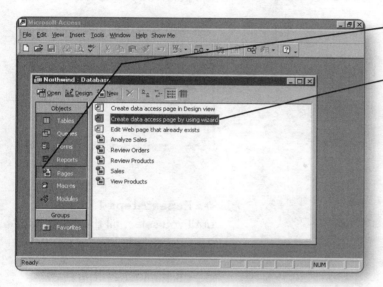

1. **Click** on the **Pages button** in the main database window.

2. **Double-click** on **Create data access page by using wizard** within the database window. The Page Wizard will open.

Selecting Fields

In the second step, you choose the specific fields to place in your page, including the table or query in which they are located.

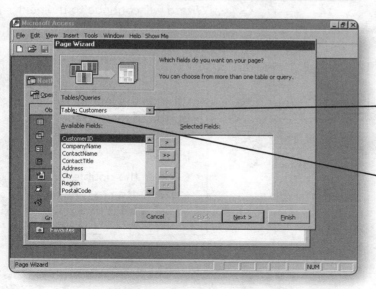

1. **Click** on the **down arrow** to the right of the Tables/Queries list box. A menu will appear.

2. **Click** on the **table or query** from which you want to select your page field. A list of the fields for that table/query will appear in the Available Fields list box.

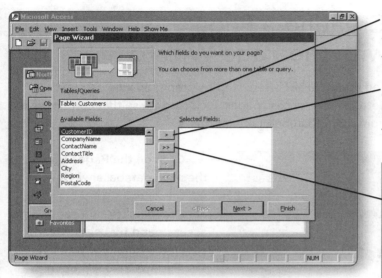

3. Choose the **first field** you want to include in your page from the Available Fields list.

4. Click on the **right arrow button**. The field will move to the Selected Fields list.

TIP

Click on the double right arrow button to include all available fields in your page.

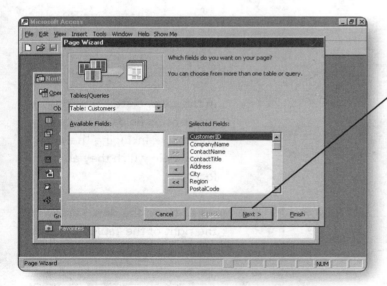

5. Repeat steps 1 through **4** until you select all the fields you want to include in your page.

6. Click on **Next**. The Page Wizard will continue to the next step.

TIP

Click on the left arrow button to remove the selected field from the page.

Click on the double left arrow button to remove all fields from your page.

Creating Groupings

In Access 2000, you can create page groupings based on one or several fields.

CAUTION

Creating groupings on a data access page makes the page read-only. If you create groupings, users will be able to view the page, but they won't be able to enter data.

1. Click on the **field** on which you want to group from the list of available fields.

2. Click on the **right arrow button**. The selected field will display in blue bold text in the preview box to the right.

3. Repeat steps 1 and **2** until you select all the fields on which you want to group.

4. Click on **Next** to continue.

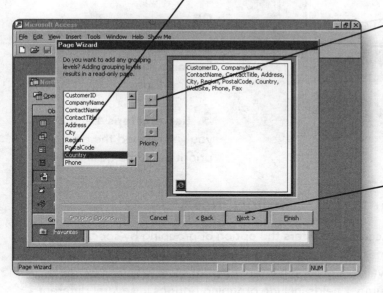

TIP

To remove a field grouping, click on the field name, then click on the left arrow button.

Changing the Grouping Priority

In the preview window, the grouping level fields display in blue bold text and are listed in order of grouping priority, with each subsequent level slightly indented. The order is based on the order in which you specify grouping levels, but you can easily change it.

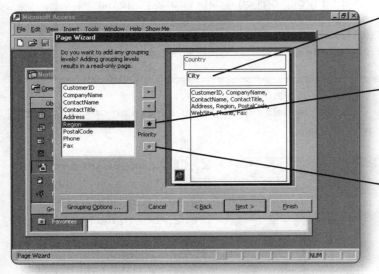

1. **Click** on the **grouping field** in the preview box whose priority you want to change.

2a. **Click** on the **up arrow button** to move this field to a higher priority.

OR

2b. **Click** on the **down arrow button** to move this field to a lower priority.

3. **Repeat steps 1** and **2** until you've changed the grouping priorities to the desired order.

Setting Grouping Intervals

Access also offers the option of grouping by specified intervals. Depending on the data type of the field, the available grouping interval options will vary. For example, number fields include grouping options in several different multiples and text fields include grouping options based on letter.

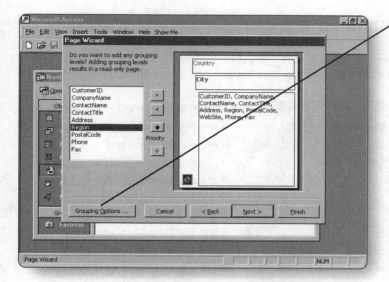

1. Click on the **Grouping Options button**. The Grouping Intervals dialog box will open.

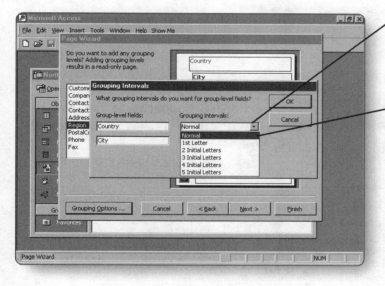

2. Click on the **down arrow** to the right of the Grouping intervals list box. A menu will appear.

3. Click on the **interval** you want. The interval will appear in the list box.

4. Repeat steps 2 and 3 until you set all grouping intervals.

5. Click on **OK**.

NOTE

Grouping intervals are only available for fields on which you've already specified a grouping level.

Specifying a Sort Order

Using the Page Wizard, you can sort up to four different fields in either ascending (the default) or descending order.

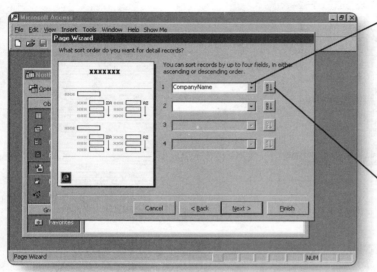

1. Click on the **down arrow** to the right of the first field. A menu will appear.

2. Click on the **first field** on which you want to sort your page. The ascending sort order will be automatically applied.

3. Click on the **AZ button** to change the sort order to descending, if desired.

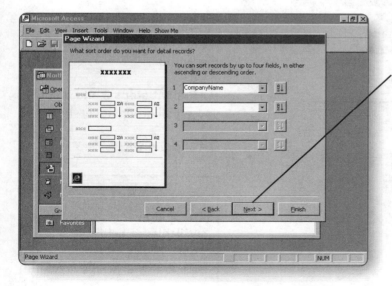

4. Repeat steps 1, 2, and 3 until you select all sort orders.

5. Click on **Next** to continue.

Finishing the Page

In the final step of the Page Wizard, you'll create a page title and select the view you want to use when opening the page for the first time.

1. **Enter** a **name** for your page in the text box.

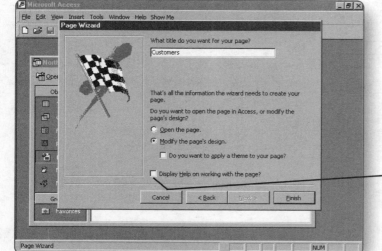

2a. **Click** on the **Open the page option button** to open the page in Page View.

OR

2b. **Click** on the **Modify the page's design option button** to open the page in Design View.

3. **Click** on the **Do you want to apply a theme to your page? check box** if you want to open the Theme dialog box when you finish your page. You can apply a design theme, similar to a style, in this dialog box.

> ### CAUTION
>
> You must choose the Modify the page's design option above if you want to apply a theme.

4. **Click** on the **Display Help on working with the page check box** if you want to display a help window when you open the page.

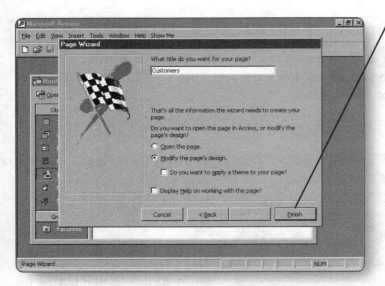

5. Click on **Finish**. The page will save as an HTML file and open based on your instructions in step 2.

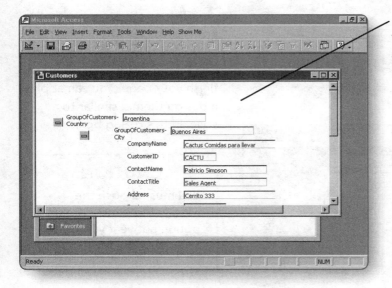

If you open your page in Page View, you'll see exactly how it will look on the Web.

If you choose the option to modify the page's design, it will open in Design View. Design View includes space for you to enter a title and body text. Click on the areas that prompt you with "Click here and type title text" and "click here and type body text" and enter the desired text.

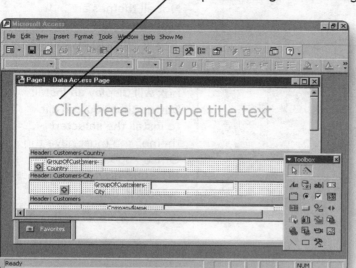

Adding a Theme

If you click the Do you want to apply a theme to your page? check box on the final step of the Page Wizard, the Theme dialog box will open before displaying your page in Design View. A theme is similar to a report or form style and includes a group of headings, bullets, and hyperlinks that blend together.

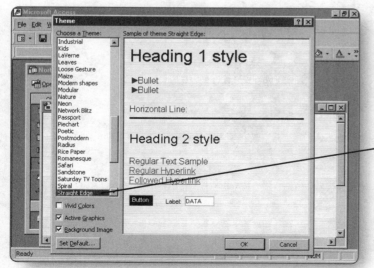

1. Click on the **theme** you want to apply from the Choose a Theme list. A sample of the theme will display on the right side of the dialog box.

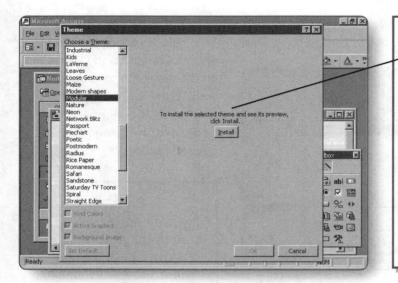

CAUTION

Not all themes are available upon initial installation. If you choose a theme that isn't installed yet, the preview box will display an Install button that you can click to install the selected theme. You must have the Office 2000 CD in your CD-ROM drive to complete this installation.

2. Click on the **Set Default button** to set the selected theme as your default theme for all future pages.

3. Click on **OK**. The data access page will open in Design View.

Previewing Your Data Access Page

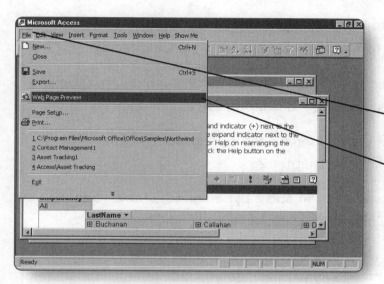

You can preview what your data access page will look like on the Web from either Page View or Design View.

1. Click on **File**. The File menu will appear.

2. Click on **Web Page Preview**.

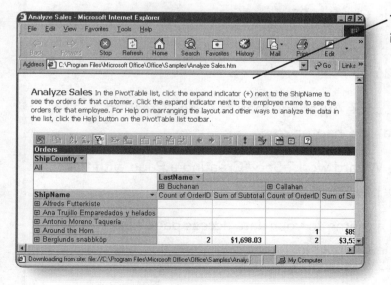

The data access page will open in Internet Explorer.

Part VIII Review Questions

1. What are the types of hyperlinks you can add to a table? *See "Adding Hyperlinks to a Table in Design View" in Chapter 25*

2. What are the four parts of a hyperlink you can enter in a table? See "Entering Hyperlinks in Tables" in Chapter 25

3. How can you be sure your hyperlink will work properly? See "Testing Your Hyperlink" in Chapter 25

4. What is the second way you can add a hyperlink to a table? See "Adding Hyperlink Columns in Datasheet View" in Chapter 25

5. How do you include a hyperlink in a form? See "Adding a Hyperlink Label to a Form" in Chapter 25

6. How do you include an e-mail address in a table? See "Linking to an E-mail Address" in Chapter 25

7. What's a data access page? See "Understanding Data Access Pages" in Chapter 26

8. When should you use the AutoPage feature? See "Creating a Columnar AutoPage" in Chapter 26

9. How does the Page Wizard work? See "Creating a Page with the Page Wizard" in Chapter 26

10. Where can you add a theme to your data access page? See "Adding a Theme" in Chapter 26

PART IX

Appendixes

A

Office 2000 Installation

Installing Office 2000 is typically very quick and easy. In this appendix, you'll learn how to:

- Install Office 2000 on your computer
- Choose which Office components you want to install
- Detect and repair problems
- Reinstall Office
- Add and remove components
- Uninstall Office 2000 completely
- Install content from other Office CDs

Installing the Software

The installation program for the Office 2000 programs is automatic. In most cases, you can simply follow the instructions onscreen.

NOTE

When you insert the Office 2000 CD for the first time, you may see a message that the installer has been updated, prompting you to restart your system. Do so, and when you return to Windows after restarting, remove the CD and reinsert it so that the Setup program starts up automatically again.

---

1. Insert the **Office 2000 CD-ROM** into your computer's CD-ROM drive. The Windows Installer will start and the Customer Information dialog box will open.

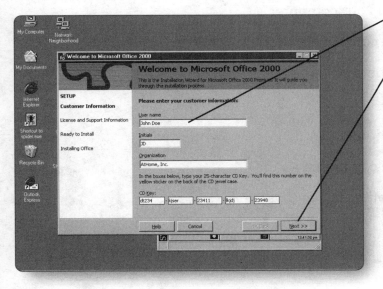

2. Type all of the **information** requested.

3. Click on **Next**. The End User License Agreement will appear.

NOTE

You'll find the CD Key number on a sticker on the back of the Office CD jewel case.

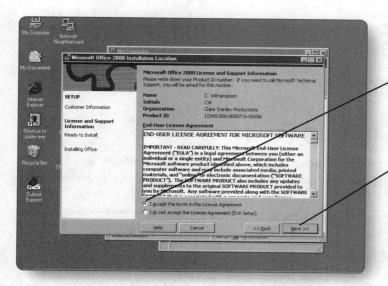

4. **Read** the **License Agreement**.

5. **Click** on the **I accept the terms in the License Agreement option button**. The option will be selected.

6. **Click** on **Next**. The Ready To Install dialog box will open.

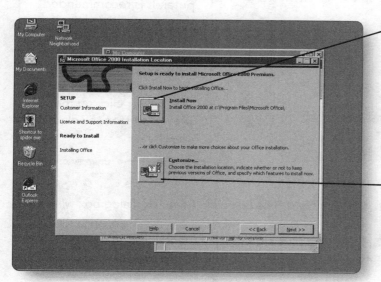

7a. **Click** on the **Install Now button.** Use this option to install Office on your computer with the default settings. This is the recommended installation for most users.

OR

7b. **Click** on the **Customize button**, if you want to choose which components to install or where to install them. The Installation Location dialog box will open. Then see the next section, "Choosing Components," for guidance.

8. **Wait** while the **Office software** installs on your computer. When the setup has completed, the Installer Information box will open.

9. Click on **Yes**. The Setup Wizard will restart your computer. After your computer has restarted, Windows will update your system settings and then finish the Office installation and configuration process.

Choosing Components

If you selected option 7b in the previous section, you have the choice of installing many different programs and components.

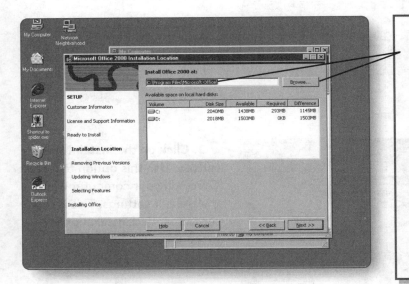

NOTE

For a custom installation, you have the option of placing Office in a different location on your computer. It is recommended that you use the default installation location. If you want to install Office in a different directory, type the directory path in the text box or click on the Browse button to select a directory.

1. Click on **Next**. The Selecting Features dialog box will open.

2. Click on a **plus sign (+)** to expand a list of features. The features listed under the category will appear.

3. Click on the **down arrow (▼)** to the right of the hard drive icon. A menu of available installation options for the feature will appear.

4. Click on the **button** next to the individual option, and choose a setting for that option:

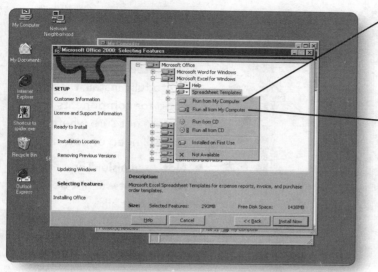

● **Run from My Computer**. The component will be fully installed, so that you will not need the Office CD in the CD-ROM drive to use it.

● **Run all from My Computer**. The selected component and all the components subordinate to it will be fully installed.

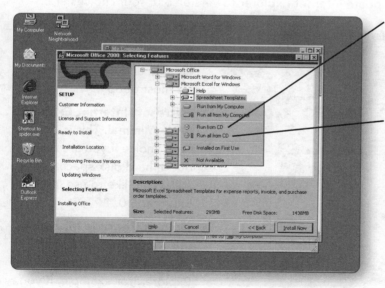

● **Run from CD**. The component will be installed, but you will need to have the Office CD in the CD-ROM drive to use it.

● **Run all from CD**. The selected component and all the components subordinate to it will need to have the Office CD in the CD-ROM drive to use it.

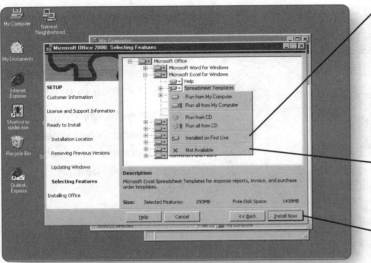

- **Installed on First Use**. The first time you try to activate the component, you will be prompted to insert the Office CD to fully install it. This is good for components that you are not sure whether you will need or not.

- **Not Available**. The component will not be installed at all.

5. Click on **Install Now**. The Installing dialog box will open.

In a Custom installation, you'll be asked whether you want to update Internet Explorer to version 5.0. Your choices are:

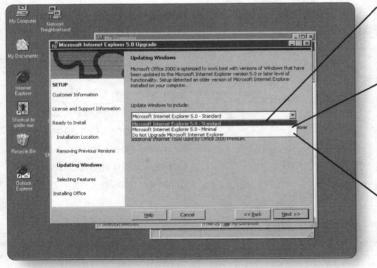

- **Microsoft Internet Explorer 5.0—Standard**. This is the default, and the right choice for most people.

- **Microsoft Internet Explorer 5.0—Minimal**. This is the right choice if you are running out of hard disk space but still would like to use Internet Explorer 5.0.

- **Do Not Upgrade Microsoft Internet Explorer**. Use this if you don't want Internet Explorer (for example, if you always use another browser such as Netscape Navigator, or if you have been directed by your system administrator not to install Internet Explorer 5).

Working with Maintenance Mode

Maintenance Mode is a feature of the Setup program. Whenever you run the Setup program again, after the initial installation, Maintenance Mode starts automatically. It enables you to add or remove features, repair your Office installation (for example, if files have become corrupted), and remove Office completely. There are several ways to rerun the Setup program (and thus enter Maintenance Mode):

- Reinsert the Office 2000 CD. The Setup program may start automatically.

- If the Setup program does not start automatically, double-click on the CD icon in the My Computer window.

- If double-clicking on the CD icon doesn't work, right-click on the CD icon and click on Open from the shortcut menu. Then double-click on the Setup.exe file in the list of files that appears.

- From the Control Panel in Windows, click on the Add/ Remove Programs button. Then on the Install/Uninstall tab, click on Microsoft Office 2000 in the list, and finally, click on the Add/Remove button.

After entering Maintenance Mode, choose the button for the activity you want. Each option is briefly described in the following sections.

Repairing or Reinstalling Office

If an Office program is behaving strangely, or refuses to work, chances are good that a needed file has become corrupted. But which file? You have no way of knowing, so you can't fix the problem yourself.

If this happens, you can either repair Office or completely reinstall it. Both options are accessed from the Repair Office button in Maintenance Mode.

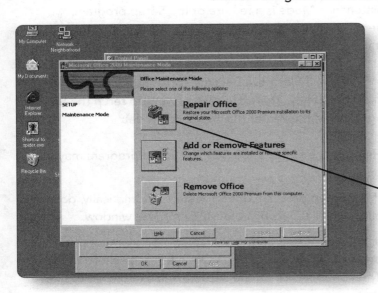

1. Click on the **Repair Office button** in Maintenance Mode.

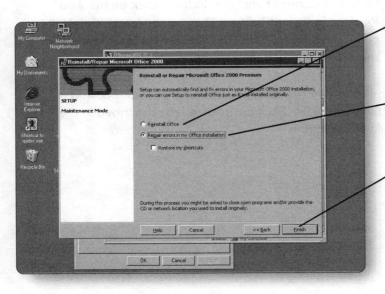

2a. Click on **Reinstall Office** to repeat the last installation.

OR

2b. Click on Repair errors in my Office installation to simply fix what's already in place.

3. Click on **Finish**. The process will start.

> ### TIP
> You can also repair individual Office programs by opening the Help menu in each program and clicking on Detect and Repair. This works well if you are sure that one certain program is causing the problem, and it's quicker than asking the Setup program to check all of the installed programs.

Adding and Removing Components

Adding and removing components works just like selecting the components initially.

1. **Click** on the **Add or Remove Features button** in Maintenance Mode. The Update Features window will appear. This window works exactly the same as the window you saw in the "Choosing Components" section earlier in this appendix.

> ### NOTE
> Some features will attempt to automatically install themselves as you are working. If you have set a feature to be installed on first use, attempt to access that feature. You will be prompted to insert your Office 2000 CD, and the feature will be installed without further prompting.

Removing Office from Your PC

In the unlikely event that you should need to remove Office from your PC completely, click on Remove Office from the Maintenance Mode screen. Then follow the prompts to remove it from your system.

After removing Office, you will probably have a few remnants left behind that the Uninstall routine didn't catch. For example, there will probably still be a Microsoft Office folder in your Program Files folder or wherever you installed the program. You can delete that folder yourself.

CAUTION

If you plan to reinstall Office later, and you have created any custom templates, toolbars, or other items, you may want to leave the Microsoft Office folder alone, so that those items will be available to you after you reinstall.

Installing Content from Other Office CDs

Depending on the version of Office you bought, you may have more than one CD in your package. CD 1 contains all the basic Office components, such as Word, Outlook, PowerPoint, Excel, Access, and Internet Explorer. It may be the only CD you need to use.

The other CDs contain extra applications that come with the specific version of Office you purchased. They may include Publisher, FrontPage, a language pack, or a programmer and developer resource kit. Each of these discs has its own separate installation program.

The additional CDs should start their Setup programs automatically when you insert the disk in your drive. If not, browse the CD's content in My Computer or Windows Explorer and double-click on the Setup.exe file that you find on it.

B

Using Keyboard Shortcuts

Access 2000 includes numerous keyboard shortcuts listed on the right side of several of the menus; you may have even started using some of these. Access also has many other keyboard shortcuts, which help make using the software even easier and more convenient. Shortcuts enable you to execute commands without using the mouse to activate menus. In this appendix, you'll learn how to:

- Get up to speed with frequently used keyboard shortcuts
- Use keyboard combinations to edit text and data

General Shortcuts

Access includes many common shortcuts that you can use in several parts of the program, such as in the Database Window, Datasheet View, Form View, etc. The following table lists a number of these general shortcuts.

TIP

Most Windows applications share the same keyboard combinations to execute common commands. Once you get accustomed to using some of these keyboard shortcuts in Access, try them out on some of the other Microsoft Office programs.

To execute this command	Do this
Display the Office Assistant	Press F1
Create a new database	Press Ctrl+N
Open an existing database	Press Ctrl+O
Save the current object	Press Ctrl+S
Open the Save As dialog box	Press F12
Print the selected object	Press Ctrl+P
Undo the previous action	Press Ctrl+Z

Datasheet View Shortcuts

You can use shortcut keys to easily navigate in Datasheet View, as illustrated in this table.

To execute this command	Do this
Go to the next field	Press Tab or Right Arrow
Go to the last field in the current record	Press End
Return to the previous field	Press Shift+Tab or the Left Arrow
Go to the first field in the current record	Press Home
Go to the next record	Press the Down Arrow
Go to the last record	Press Ctrl+Down Arrow
Go to the last field in the last record	Press Ctrl+End
Return to the previous record	Press the Up Arrow
Return to the current field in the first record	Press Ctrl+Up Arrow
Return to the first field in the first record	Press Ctrl+Home
Move down one screen	Press Page Down
Move up one screen	Press Page Up
Move one screen right	Press Ctrl+Page Down
Move one screen left	Press Ctrl+Page Up
Go to the record number box	Press F5

Form View Shortcuts

When you're in Form View you can use a variety of different shortcuts, many of which are similar to the ones you use in Datasheet View. This table lists the most common shortcuts.

To execute this command	Do this
Go to the next field	Press Tab
Return to the previous field	Press Shift+Tab
Go to the last field in the current record	Press End
Go to the first field in the current record	Press Home
Go to the next record	Press Ctrl+Page Down
Return to the previous record	Press Ctrl+Page Up
Go to the last field in the last record	Press Ctrl+End
Return to the first field in the first record	Press Ctrl+Home
Move down one page	Press Page Down
Move up one page	Press Page Up
Go to the record number box	Press F5

Print Preview Shortcuts

Print Preview also has similar shortcuts. These include the shortcuts listed in the table below.

To execute this command	Do this
Open the Print dialog box	Press P or Ctrl+P
Open the Page Setup dialog box	Press S
Zoom in and out of the page	Press Z
Cancel Print Preview	Press C or Esc
Scroll down in small increments	Press the Down Arrow
Scroll up in small increments	Press the Up Arrow
Scroll to the right in small increments	Press the Right Arrow
Scroll to the left in small increments	Press the Left Arrow
Scroll down one full screen	Press Page Down
Scroll up one full screen	Press Page Up
Go to the bottom of the page	Press Ctrl+Down Arrow
Go to the top of the page	Press Ctrl+Up Arrow
Go to the right edge of the page	Press End or Ctrl+Right Arrow
Go to the left edge of the page	Press Home or Ctrl+Left Arrow
Go to the lower-right corner of the page	Press Ctrl+End
Go to the upper-left corner of the page	Press Ctrl+Home
Go to the page number box	Press F5

Text and Data Shortcuts

When you need to enter and edit extensive amount of data, such as in tables or forms, you'll be glad to use as many shortcuts as possible.

Selection Shortcuts

Before you can edit the text in your Access tables, forms, and reports, you'll need to select it. This table shows you how to use keyboard combinations to select text.

To execute this command	Do this
Select the character to the right of the cursor	Press Shift+Right Arrow
Select the character to the left of the cursor	Press Shift+Left Arrow
Select the entire word to the right	Press Ctrl+Shift+Right Arrow
Select the entire word to the left	Press Ctrl+Shift+Left Arrow
Select the next field	Press Tab

Editing Shortcuts

Once you select the text to which you want to make the editing changes, apply one of the combinations in the following table.

To execute this command	Do this
Delete the character to the left of the cursor	Press Backspace
Delete the character to the right of the cursor	Press Delete
Delete the word to the left of the cursor	Press Ctrl+Backspace

To execute this command	Do this
Delete the word to the right	Press Ctrl+Delete
Cut the selected object/text	Press Ctrl+X
Copy the selected object/text	Press Ctrl+C
Paste the selected object/text	Press Ctrl+V
Delete the selected object/text	Press Delete
Rename the selected object/text	Press F2
Search for a word or words	Press Ctrl+F
Replace a word or words	Press Ctrl+H
Undo an edit	Press Ctrl+Z or Alt+Backspace
Undo changes in the current field or record	Press Esc
Check spelling	Press F7
Add a new record	Press Ctrl+Plus Sign (+)
Delete the current record	Press Ctrl+Minus Sign (-)
Save changes to the current record	Press Shift+Enter
Insert the same value from the previous record	Press Ctrl+Apostrophe (')

Menu Command Shortcuts

Finally, you may also want to use shortcut keys to activate menu commands instead of using the mouse. Use the shortcuts in this table to access menus.

To execute this command	Do this
Activate the menu bar	Press F10
Display a shortcut menu	Press Shift+F10
Display the program menu	Press Alt+Spacebar
Select the next menu command	Press the Down Arrow
Go back to the previous menu command	Press the Up Arrow
Select the next option on the menu bar	Press the Right Arrow
Go back to the previous option on the menu bar	Press the Left Arrow
Close the visible menu	Press Alt
Close a submenu	Press Esc

Glossary

Address. The URL of the Web site to which you want to link. An example of an address is http://www.microsoft.com.

AutoForm. A basic automated form in either a columnar, tabular, or datasheet format.

AutoFormat. A way to automatically apply specific fonts, colors, and borders to a selected form or report.

AutoNumber. A data type which stores a unique incremented number for every record in a table.

AutoReport. A basic automated report in either a columnar or tabular format.

Browser. An external software program used to access and view World Wide Web pages. Microsoft Internet Explorer and Netscape Navigator are examples of browsers.

Check box. A control that lets you choose a particular option. A check mark in the check box indicates that the option is selected; no check mark indicates that it is not selected.

Click on. A way to perform an action by using the mouse to select a button, menu, or dialog box option.

Clipboard. A Windows holding area for transferring data.

Close button. A button you use to exit a dialog box, window, or Access itself.

Combo box. A control that contains a drop-down list from which you can select one of the listed values or enter a specific value not on the list.

Control. An object you place on a report or form. Text boxes, combo boxes, and option buttons are all examples of controls.

Criteria. Query and filter conditions that narrow the selected records or data.

Crosstab query. A query that summarizes information in a spreadsheet format by crosstabulating data.

Current record. The unique selected record that you can use or modify.

Data Entry mode. A mode that displays a blank table or form in which to enter data; temporarily hides all previously entered records from view.

Data access page. An Access form or report designed for the Web.

Data type. A table field property that specifies the type of data you'll store in that field. Text, number, and date/time are examples of data types.

Database. A collection of information. In Access, objects such as forms, tables, reports, and queries make up a database.

Database window. A window that contains six tabs, each corresponding to one of the six objects that make up an Access database.

Datasheet View. A view that displays table data in rows and columns, as in a spreadsheet.

Default. A value that automatically displays in a field or control.

Design grid. The bottom portion of the Select Query window in which you specify query criteria.

Design View. A view that allows you to design or modify the selected report, table, form, or query.

Detail query. A select query that contains all fields in all records.

Dialog box. A box that displays when you perform another action, such as clicking on a button or menu option. A dialog box can either provide information or let you select additional options.

Display text. The text you want to display in a hyperlink field in a table.

Edit mode. A mode that allows you to enter data in a table or form; adds records to the end of existing records.

Field. A column in a table. An individual field relates specifically to the record with which it intersects.

Form. A database object you use to enter, view, and edit table data.

Filter by form. A feature that lets you filter based on more than one criterion.

Filter by selection. A feature that lets you select specific data in a table open in Datasheet View and then apply a basic filter.

Form section. A way to divide a form; an Access form can have detail, form header, page header, page footer, and form footer sections.

Form View. A view in which you can enter data in a form.

Hyperlink. In Access, a field data type that stores a link to a Web page or other object.

Hypertext Markup Language (HTML). A method of marking up or formatting documents for the World Wide Web.

Import. A method of transferring data from another source, such as a spreadsheet, into an Access table.

Internet. An international network of millions of computers.

Intranet. An internal corporate or organizational network that uses Internet technology.

Join lines. Lines in the Select Query window that relate data in one table to data in another.

Label. A control that displays descriptive text such as a title or caption.

Landscape. A page orientation that prints reports in a horizontal format.

List box. A control that contains a drop-down list from which you can select one of the listed values.

Menu bar. The horizontal bar located directly below the Access title bar that includes menu names.

Menu. A command list that displays when you click on a menu name on the menu bar.

Navigation buttons. Buttons that display in Datasheet and Form views that let you move to the first, last, next, and preceding records.

Office Assistant. A help feature that answers users' questions.

Option button. A small button that precedes a text option on an Access form; part of an option group. Sometimes referred to as a radio button.

Option group. A control that lets you choose one of several displayed options, preceded by option buttons, check boxes, or toggle buttons.

Portrait. A page orientation that prints reports in a vertical format.

Primary key. One or more table fields that serve as a unique tag for each table record; this unique key relates the records in the current table to records in other tables.

Print Preview. A view that displays a report as it will look when you print it.

Query. A database object that extracts specific information from a database; it can also perform an action on this data.

Record. A row in a table.

Report. A database object that presents or analyzes database information in a printed format.

Report section. A way to divide a report; an Access report can have detail, report header, page header, page footer, report footer, group header, and group footer sections.

ScreenTip. A tip that appears when you position the mouse pointer over a toolbar button or particular part of the screen.

Select query. A query that selects specific information from a database.

Sort. A command that organizes selected data in either ascending or descending order.

Style. A method of formatting objects using the same fonts, backgrounds, and colors.

Subaddress. The exact location in a Web page or document to which you want to link.

Subdatasheet. A datasheet within a datasheet that displays related table data for each individual record.

Summary query. A select query that summarizes information.

Table. A database object that serves as a collector of information about a related subject, organized by fields and records.

Text box. A control that you place on a form or report to display table or query data.

Title bar. The horizontal bar located directly above the menu bar, which displays the name of the open window.

Toolbar. A horizontal bar located below the menu bar, which includes toolbar buttons that you click on to perform a specific action.

Toolbox. A toolbar that contains a series of buttons you use to create form or report controls.

Uniform Resource Locator (URL). The address of the Internet document, Web page, or object to which you want to link. An example of a URL is http://www.microsoft.com.

View. A window that lets you use an Access object in a particular way.

Wizard. An automated feature that guides you step-by-step through a process. In Access, you can use wizards to create databases, tables, reports, forms, and queries, for example.

World Wide Web. A graphical Internet environment accessed with a browser and organized with Web sites comprised of text, graphics, sound, and video.

Zoom. A way to reduce or enlarge the area you view in Print Preview.

Index

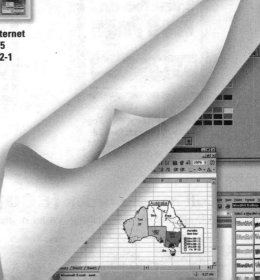